Riding the routes of the Great War

in the North, the Pas-de-Calais, the Somme, the Aisne and Belgium

VÉLO GUIDE

Maps

Patrick Mérienne

Editions OUEST-FRANCE

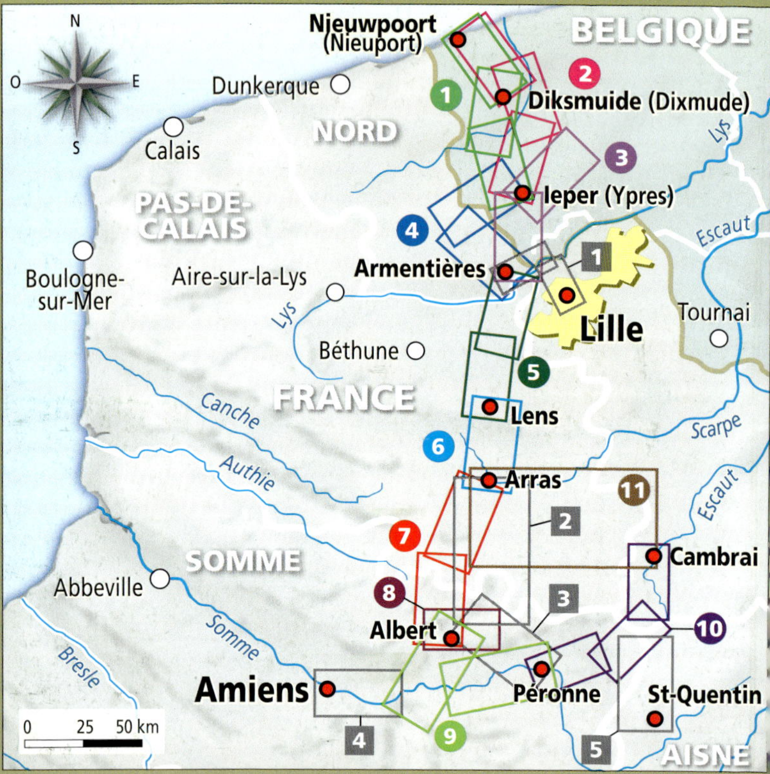
N
O
E
S
Nieuwpoort
(Nieuport)
BELGIQUE
Dunkerque
1
2
Diksmuide (Dixmude)
Calais
NORD
Lys
3
PAS-DE-CALAIS
Ieper (Ypres)
4
Escaut
1
Boulogne-sur-Mer
Aire-sur-la-Lys
Armentières
Lys
Tournai
Lille
Béthune
5
FRANCE
Canche
Lens
Scarpe
6
Authie
Arras
11
Escaut
2
7
SOMME
Cambrai
Abbeville
8
3
Albert
10
Somme
Bresle
Amiens
Péronne
St-Quentin
0 25 50 km
4
9
5
AISNE

Contents

Introduction

This book sets out to explore memorial sites, trenches, tunnels, craters and military cemeteries – all silent witnesses of the Great War that raged over Europe a century ago. It invites readers to ride along the old Western Front on quiet country lanes, away from busy roads and heavy traffic.

Just months after the outbreak of World War I, the German advance came to a standstill. Both sides dug in along a winding line of fortified trenches that stretched from Nieuwpoort on the Belgian coast through the flat fields of Flanders, the hills of Artois, the rolling plains of the Somme and on to the Swiss border.

This book covers the old front line from the North Sea in Belgium to the Saint-Quentin Canal and tells the stories of the major offensives that took place in the mud of Ypres and Passchendaele, the limestone rocks of Artois and the valley and hills of the Somme.

Although the focus of the book is a series of battlefields, the wide variety of landscapes and the geographical make-up of northern France and the western part of Belgium, little known among bike riders, will often surprise you.

Safety always comes first! Rather than taking the fastest routes to historical sites, we have given priority to slow roads. In a bid to offer cyclists maximum flexibility, the stages can be combined to devise a centre-based itinerary that brings you back to your base after 100, 200 or 300km.

Riding the routes of the Great War

How to use this guide

Handy hints and advice

An atypical itinerary

Cycling the Western Front takes you along cart tracks, trails, paths, towpaths and major and minor roads. Given the nature of the subject, at times your itinerary may seem somewhat random. You will follow rivers, cross canals, span open plains, climb steep slopes and travel through neighbourhoods and busy city centres. The logic behind the chosen itinerary is always the course of the war.

The general concept

This guide presents 4 stages in Belgium and 7 stages and 5 special outings in Picardy. These two series of centre-based stages are linked by a two-stage journey in Nord-Pas-de-Calais, between Armentières and Arras. The total adds up to 720km (450 miles) of routes which are accessible from the major cities in the north of France and from Brussels, Paris and London via the Eurostar international train station, Lille Europe.

Tailor-made journeys

Each stage covers a specific subject so that you can organise your trip and ride two to four stages at a time, planning your rides around a town or city or a particular area of interest. Since the stages are laid out in loops, you can travel light as you will return to your hotel or car at the end of your journey.

Open to everyone

The topography and geography of the land between the Belgian coast and Saint-Quentin do not require you to be a trained athlete. The routes are open to everyone. If the climb up the hill at Notre-Dame de Lorette is a bit of a challenge, you can simply walk 600 yards up to the top of the hill before getting on your bike again. The distance of each stage is roughly 50km (35 to 40 miles). Only stage 9 is substantially longer, but the town of Corbie and the city of Amiens (stage 4) mean that you can easily split your journey over two days.

Signposts at junctions or knooppunten (knots)

On the Belgian side of the border you will notice posts bearing a number and sign. These refer to the dense network of cycle routes that are all registered and mapped. Every junction where three or more routes join is known as a knot or *knooppunt* and has a specific number that is marked on a post. For the first four stages, reference will be made to the numbers on these posts that you find on your path. The signs are green on a white board; they are easy to spot and can be useful to help you find your way. On the French side of the border you will follow the signs on the departmental roads (B-roads), but the signposts of the Commonwealth War Graves Commission and its German counterpart also serve as good indicators.

Safety

Your journey will frequently deviate from signposted cycle routes and at times you will even have to negotiate your way across busy

city centre junctions. Where feasible your itinerary will lead you away from the main traffic as quickly as possible and may seem rather complicated. Although priority is given to slow roads, in most cases you will have to share the road with motorised vehicles. Wearing a cycle helmet is not compulsory in France, but as cycle helmets reduce the risk of head injury by 75% we strongly advise the use of a helmet. In addition, you may come across unexploded ammunition on remote country roads. The risk of an explosion is rare but real, and accidents do happen. You should therefore avoid touching or handling any ammunition.

The towns and cities

The comments on the towns and cities where the stages start or end only refer to their role during the First World War. Since the internet provides up-to-date information on hotels, B&Bs and restaurants, you will not find a review of these facilities in this guide. An exception has been made for a handful of unique places that could easily be overlooked and do have that little extra something!

Stage 1

From Ypres *(Ieper)* to Nieuwpoort via Diksmuide

The Belgian sector of the Western Front

42km

In this first stage you will explore the flat countryside of Flanders by following the towpath along the Ypres-Yser Canal and the banks of the river Yser to Diksmuide. After 42km you will join the North Sea at the Belgian coast. The towpath is a popular cycle path used by school children on their way to school during the week and by recreational cyclists at weekends. You will see the posts for the Belgian cycle network all the way to Nieuwpoort.

The Cloth Hall in Ypres (Ieper) is where your journey begins…

Ypres and the Ypres Salient

In the 12th century the town of Ypres was the centre of the linen trade in Europe. But by the turn of the 14th century, with the Hundred Years War and the decline of the weaving industry, the Flanders linen trade was on the wane. The population of Ypres shrank from 40,000 in 1260 to just 17,000 in 1907.

When the German advance had come to a halt in 1914, the continuous lines of trenches formed the Western Front. In Flanders an outward bulge in the lines around the town of Ypres became known as the Ypres Salient, where the enemy held the high ground and observed every Allied movement. The town was shelled at will and after four years Ypres was reduced to rubble.

The Schlieffen Plan

The invasion of Belgium was an inevitable element in the German plan that aimed to defeat the French using an envelopment strategy. By saving Paris, the French saved France and ended the speedy German offensive. The opponents then attempted to outflank each other through north-eastern France. Arras was not occupied but Vimy Ridge did fall into German hands.

The importance of Belgian and French ports such as Dunkirk in supplying the Allies was recognised at the time. The aim of retaining control of the French coast was achieved in the battles fought in Artois. In Flanders, however, neither side could gain the upper hand. This produced a continuous line of trench fortifications.

Reconstructed trench systems amidst the craters at Vimy Ridge.

The Belgians fall back behind the Yser

After the siege of Antwerp the remnants of the Belgian army were pushed back west and made a stand behind the river Yser, over a 35km stretch from the coast to Diksmuide. The Germans captured advanced posts and reached the Yser. Diksmuide finally fell into German hands. The Germans launched another major attack on the Yser on 30 October 1914. The attack punched through the Belgian second line and reached Ramskapelle. The Belgians opened the sluices at Nieuwpoort during high tides, steadily raising the water level until an impassable flooded area was created, stretching as far south as Diksmuide. The German army failed to defeat the Belgian army.

The Belgian Monument.

The First Battle of Ypres

Taking the ports of Calais and Dunkirk was the only option open to the Germans to prevent the Allies from shipping troops and supplies across the English Channel to the continent. Ypres was the last major obstacle on the German advance to the French coast; it offered geographical protection for the Allied ports and was strategically vital. The Ypres campaign became the culmination of the Race to the Sea. The opposing armies engaged in offensive operations until a massive German assault was launched in mid-October, forcing the Allies onto the strategic defensive and limiting them to counter-attacks. Diksmuide fell but Ypres was saved. By 17 November 1914 the front had been stabilised.

The Western Front

After the battle, Erich von Falkenhayn reasoned that it was no longer possible for Germany to win the war, and was saddened at the loss of vast swathes of German youth (see stage 2). The German army retreated and dug in, establishing the beginnings of a static Western Front that was to last for the next three years.

The Allies saved the Channel ports and by Christmas they held an unbroken line from the coast to Flanders, Artois and the Somme valley. The war quickly became one of attrition, which meant that with so many soldiers being killed daily, eventually the side with the most men would win the war.

The Cloth Hall in Ypres.

❶ This route starts in the market square of Ypres, at the Cloth Hall. The imposing Cloth Hall was built in the 13th century and was one of the largest commercial buildings in the Middle Ages. The renovated building now hosts the In Flanders Fields Museum (www.inflanders-fields.be), which presents the story of the First World War on the Ypres front. The Cloth Hall is an important symbol of wartime hardship and subsequent recovery – the current building, rebuilt after the war, is an exact copy of the original mediaeval building.

◆ From the Cloth Hall, follow Diksmuidestraat all the way down to the canal where you join the towpath on the left bank.

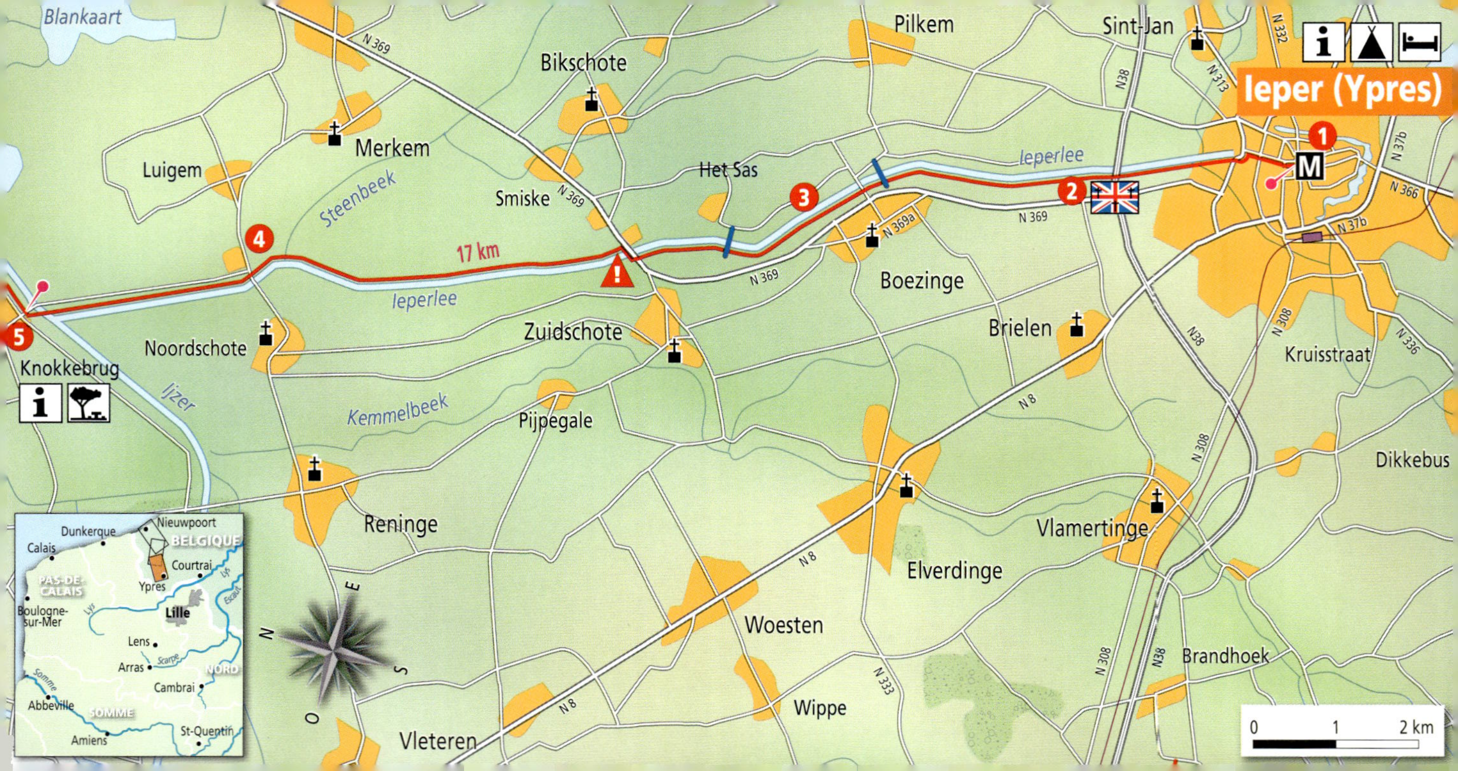
Ieper (Ypres)
Blankaart
N 369
Pilkem
Sint-Jan
N 332
N 313
N 38
Bikschote
Merkem
Luigem
Het Sas
Ieperlee
Smiske
Steenbeek
N 37b
N 366
17 km
N 369a
Boezinge
Noordschote
Zuidschote
Knokkebrug
Ijzer
Brielen
Kruisstraat
N 308
N 336
Kemmelbeek
Pijpegale
N 8
Dikkebus
Reninge
Vlamertinge
Elverdinge
Woesten
Brandhoek
N 333
Wippe
Vleteren
Nieuwpoort
Dunkerque
Calais
BELGIQUE
PAS-DE-CALAIS
Courtrai
Ypres
Boulogne-sur-Mer
Lille
Lens
Arras
Cambrai
NORD
Somme
Abbeville
SOMME
St-Quentin
Amiens
Lys
Escaut
Scarpe
N
E
S
O
0
1
2 km

◆ Under King Louis XIV this waterway was part of France's border defences. Napoleon later had it deepened and widened to make it navigable. The soil was dumped on the west bank and proved to be a valuable asset as it formed an effective barrier to stop the German advance in 1914.

John McCrae Path.

❷ After 1.8km you will come to a cobbled path that is perpendicular to the canal and leads to a WWI aid post or dressing station around 100m from the canal. During and after battles, stretcher-bearers brought hundreds of wounded soldiers to this triage post. Many have their final resting place in the adjacent Essex Farm Cemetery. Those who needed surgery were evacuated by field ambulance to casualty clearing stations and military hospitals. The second and fourth stages tell the story of these hospital sectors behind the lines.

In Flanders Fields

During the various battles, doctors worked relentlessly at the dressing stations to save soldiers. One such doctor was John McCrae, who witnessed his good friend and officer Alexis Helmer being killed by a shell burst. He committed his friend to the ground and was deeply moved. It was in writing a poem that he found a way to express his emotions and his fascination for the poppies that emerged on churned-up battlefields and hastily-dug graves. The blood-like colour of the flower made it seem like the field was pushing up the blood that was spilled in battle.

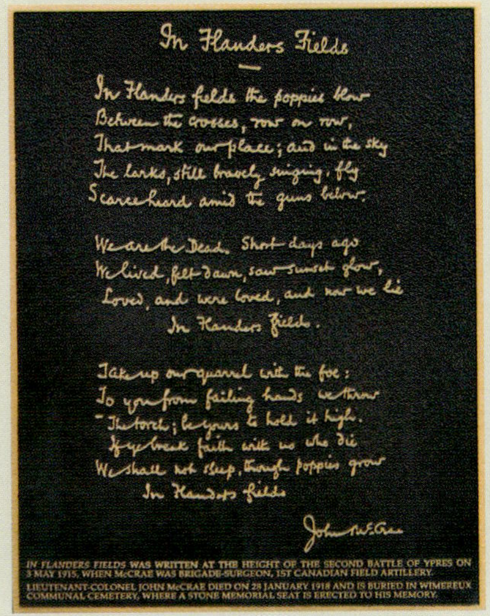

The poem.

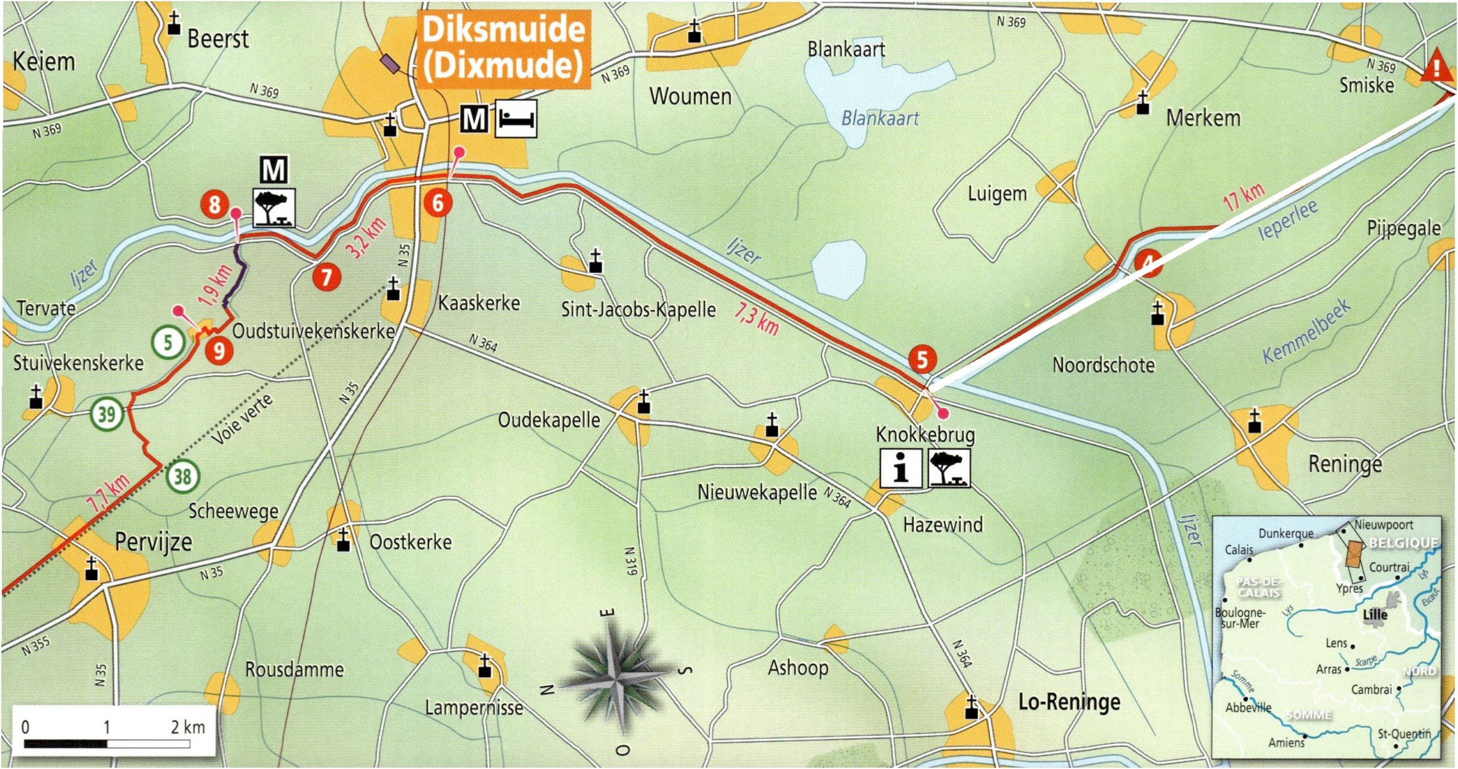
Diksmuide (Dixmude)
Keiem
Beerst
Woumen
Blankaart
Blankaart
Merkem
Smiske
Luigem
Pijpegale
Ieperlee
17 km
Ijzer
Kemmelbeek
Noordschote
Tervate
Stuivekenskerke
Oudstuivekenskerke
Kaaskerke
Sint-Jacobs-Kapelle
7,3 km
3,2 km
1,9 km
7,7 km
Voie verte
Knokkebrug
Oudekapelle
Nieuwekapelle
Hazewind
Reninge
Scheewege
Pervijze
Oostkerke
Rousdamme
Lampernisse
Ashoop
Lo-Reninge
N 369
N 35
N 364
N 319
N 355
0 1 2 km
Dunkerque
Nieuwpoort
BELGIQUE
Calais
Courtrai
PAS-DE-CALAIS
Ypres
Boulogne-sur-Mer
Lille
Lens
Arras
NORD
Cambrai
Abbeville
SOMME
Amiens
St-Quentin

Poppies, a symbol of remembrance

After the war, Anna E. Guérin, a representative of the French YMCA Secretariat, had the idea of producing and selling handmade artificial poppies as a way of raising money for orphans, widows and veterans. Madame Guérin went to visit Field Marshal Earl Douglas Haig, Chief of Staff of the British forces in France and Belgium and founder of the Royal British Legion, in person. She persuaded him to adopt the Flanders poppy as an emblem for the Legion. This was formalised in autumn 1921.

Today, the Haig Fund continues to support veterans of all conflicts and other military actions involving the British Armed Forces.

The locks at Boezinge.

❸ Return to the towpath and 4km further on you will come to a system of two sluices. In the 17th century a new canal was created with locks so that it would be navigable. These sluices were entirely destroyed during the war and it wasn't until 1933 that the first barge could sail on the canal again.

4 2km further north, when you reach the hamlet of Drie Grachten, you leave the towpath, cross the canal and follow the road on the other side for 8km. Motorised vehicles may occasionally use this road.

◆ The crossing was the scene of bitter fighting in 1915 until the Germans captured and fortified this passage. The Belgians dug in 500 yards behind the bridge. The field was then flooded and the stalemate continued.

The drawbridge and adjacent rest area.

5 At the end of the canal you cross the drawbridge and turn right onto the road along the river Yser. The plaque on the right-hand side of the drawbridge explains about local fauna and flora and tells the story of the 18th-century Fort Knokke.

6 You have 7km more to pedal on this busy road along the river Yser before you reach Diksmuide. The Belgian Peace Monument or Ijzertoren (Yser Tower) was erected in the valley of the Yser after the war and became a site of pilgrimage for all Belgians. As the Flemish push for cultural autonomy gathered pace, however, the monument was destroyed and a new tower was funded and rebuilt by the Flemish community in Belgium. When one radical political party monopolised the use of the monument to spread its controversial political views, the tower lost its original meaning and became a source of division for Belgians. Over the last two decades, efforts have been made to promote the message of peace and the tower now houses a local WWI museum commemorating the battles of the Yser.

The Peace Monument.

The French save the front

The bridge that stands 100 yards from the peace monument is where the Germans intended to cross the Yser. Belgian and French units under Colonel Alphonse Jacques defended the city and some outposts. Despite heavy losses, the Belgians and French held the town, but two weeks later fresh German assault troops were able to establish a bridgehead on the west bank of the Yser. French counter-attacks successfully recovered the west bank, but not the town. Floods later immobilised the two sides in their positions.

Monument to the French Admiral Ronarc'h in Diksmuide.

The last line of defence

As a result of the massive offensive known as the First Battle of Ypres, Diksmuide fell to the Germans, but Allied counter-attacks prevented them from establishing a foothold on the western bank there.
The Germans now shifted their focus onto a large bend in the river, north of Diksmuide, from where they were able to observe and overpower the Belgians. Eventually they managed to establish a bridgehead on the west bank and had breached the Belgian front.

Flooding the valley of the Yser

The Belgian army fell back behind the embankment of the Diksmuide-Nieuwpoort railway, supported by the French on their right flank (at Diksmuide). By flooding the farmland between the embankment and the river the Belgians created an obstacle that proved too much for the Germans to overcome. The German army failed to defeat the Belgians, who retained control over the last corner of their territory and also saved the port of Dunkirk. "Little Belgium" had stopped the German steamroller and the world's media compared it to David in his struggle against Goliath.

7 From Diksmuide you ride along the bank of the river Yser for another 2km until you reach the square red brick building that houses "Trench of Death", a Belgian visitor centre and museum.

◆ Belgian soldiers started digging a trench directly towards German positions, while the Germans had the same idea and their sappers dug a trench towards the Belgian lines. The collision was inevitable. All knew that the enemy was only yards away and was ready to charge. When confrontation came, the soldiers had to fight in hand-to-hand combat in indescribable conditions. It was virtually impossible to evacuate the wounded and deliver supplies. A support trench was dug parallel to the existing line in an attempt to improve conditions.

◆ The "Knight" machine gun post is perpendicular to the trench and its arc of fire formed a bolt that kept the line from being breached. This setting contributed to the final stalemate in this sector. This section of the Belgian defences was later preserved for its military and emotional significance. The centre is open to visitors free of charge. From the window on the first floor you can observe how the trenches followed the bends in the river.

8 From the Belgian memorial site you return to the river and ride along it for another 900m until a gravel path takes you away from the road and cuts across the lowlands to the village of Stuivekenskerke.

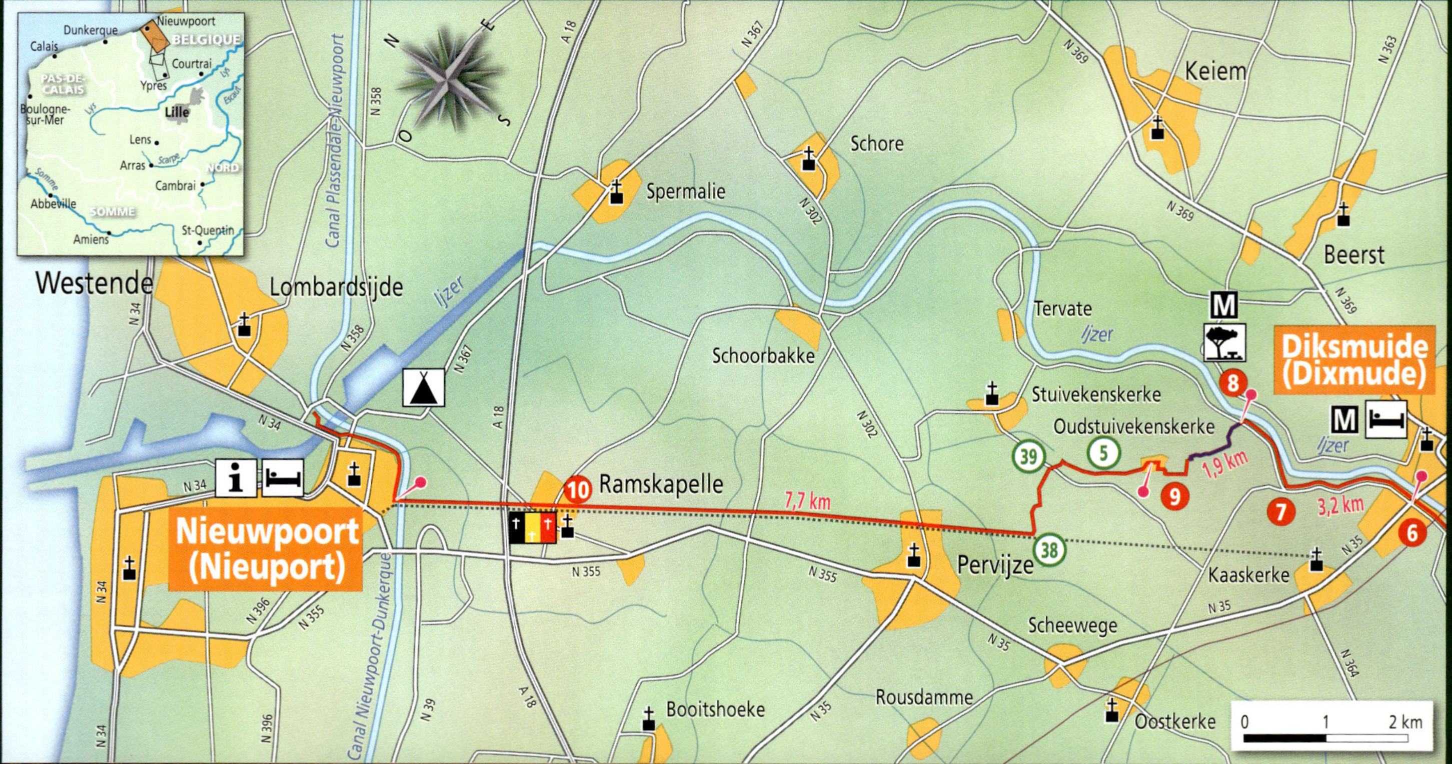
Nieuwpoort
(Nieuport)
Diksmuide
(Dixmude)
Westende
Lombardsijde
Spermalie
Schore
Keiem
Beerst
Tervate
Schoorbakke
Stuivekenskerke
Oudstuivekenskerke
Ramskapelle
Pervijze
Kaaskerke
Scheewege
Rousdamme
Booitshoeke
Oostkerke
IJzer
Canal Plassendale-Nieuwpoort
Canal Nieuwpoort-Dunkerque
7,7 km
1,9 km
3,2 km
N 34
N 358
N 367
A 18
N 302
N 369
N 363
N 355
N 396
N 39
N 35
N 364
N
E
S
O
0
1
2 km
Dunkerque
Nieuwpoort
BELGIQUE
Calais
Courtrai
PAS-DE-CALAIS
Ypres
Boulogne-sur-Mer
Lille
Lens
Arras
NORD
Cambrai
Abbeville
SOMME
Amiens
St-Quentin
Lys
Escaut
Scarpe
Somme

The Demarcation Stones

Paul Moreau-Vauthier, a veteran and sculptor, had the original idea of erecting 129 milestones to mark the 700km-long front line on 18 July 1918, the turning point of the Second Battle of the Marne. The idea was adopted by the French and Belgian automobile clubs, and Marshal Pétain was asked to make a list of the places worthy to receive a demarcation stone. The stone at the foot of the observation post is engraved with the words "Here the invader was brought to a halt" in three languages.

9 1.8km down this path is an old church tower that served as an observation post for the Belgian artillery. Two patches of higher ground in the flooded fields formed two islands in a sea of mud and water. One remained in the hands of the Belgians but the other became a German foothold. Both served as observation posts for their artillery and became the target of numerous attacks. This forms the context of the unique story of the Fighting Monk.

The Belgian observation post.

The Fighting Monk

Edouard-Martial Lekeux graduated as an artillery officer after four years at the Royal Military Academy. He was chosen to serve at the forts around Liège. But after much careful thought he decided to enter the religious order of the Franciscans. When the war broke out and his country was invaded by the Germans, he re-enlisted as Lieutenant Lekeux and was posted here at the observation tower in no man's land, where he served for 11 months without leave. People heard about his story when a member of the Belgian Government mentioned to the press that a monk was fighting as an officer in the artillery. The stained-glass window of the chapel shows a soldier dressed like a monk.

The Fighting Monk.

⑩ From the chapel you follow the signs to *knooppunt* 5, then 39 and 38, and this brings you to the embankment of the old railway that now is a cycle path named *Frontzate*. Follow the signs for Nieuwpoort and ride along the embankment that contained the flood waters and formed the last barrier of the Belgian army against the German offensives.

The Frontzate track.

The Demarcation Stone saved!

When Belgium was occupied again during the Second World War, the German authorities felt that this message was no longer correct, since 1940 marked the end of the First World War with the surrender of France to the Third Reich. A special unit was then sent out to erase the inscriptions. A local farmer did not like this idea at all so he filled a cart with manure and poured it all over the Demarcation Stone. His efforts were enough to keep the brigade of the Third Reich from erasing the inscription here, and this stone is one of just two that were left undamaged.

The Demarcation Stone.

◆ Some 5.9km further on, just before a crossing, you will come across an unusual piece of art next to a concrete observation post. It tells the story of the spontaneous truce between German, French and Belgian soldiers during the first winter of the war. When the strains of *Stille Nacht* sounded from the German trenches on Christmas morning, the Allied soldiers joined them in singing. With no officers around to tell them otherwise, the men left their trenches to greet the "others", exchange souvenirs, bury their dead and organise a religious service together. In stage 3 you will visit a second sector where there was a truce on Christmas Day.

The Christmas Truce.

◆ A series of widespread unofficial ceasefires took place along the Western Front at Christmas 1914. The truce is often seen as a symbolic moment of peace and humanity amidst one of the most violent events in human history.

◆ Should you wish to pass straight to the second stage, turn right at the steel bridge and ride to the Belgian monument that overlooks the canals, the river and the port.

Nieuwpoort

At the end of the old train track, you cross the metal bridge and enter Nieuwpoort. The name comes from the Latin *Novus Portus*, new port, and refers to the port that was constructed here in the Middle Ages.
In 1914 this town was on the path of the invaders as they marched to Dunkirk.
The complex of five sluices controls and regulates the water table in the rivers and canals of the polders, where most fields are below sea level at high tide.

Stage 2

From Nieuwpoort to Ypres *(Ieper)*

The military cemeteries behind German lines

57km

The second stage starts almost exactly where the Western Front intersected with the North Sea, where the river Yser flows out into the open sea and a complex of five locks and sluices controls and regulates the water table in the rivers and canals around the flat farmland of the polders between Ostend and Diksmuide.

When the Belgians stopped the Germans and finally halted their invasion, it marked a dramatic turning point in the war.

The park in Langemark is the perfect area for a break or a picnic.

When a battlefield becomes a lake

To flood the fields between the river Yser and the embankment where the Belgian army had its last stand, the complex system of drains, canals and sluice gates was reversed so that it would open at high tide and let the sea invade the fields occupied by the enemy. After six hours the same sluice gates had to be locked again to keep the water in. This action permanently paralysed the front line. The German army failed to defeat the Belgian army and the retention of the last corner of Belgium ended the Race to the Sea and the period of open warfare. The Germans turned their attention further south to Ypres.

❶ The series of sluices named the "Goose Foot" – for its particular shape – which regulate the flow of the river Yser and four other canals became the cornerstone of Belgium's defence as it tried to hold on to the last piece of Belgian territory.

❷ Ride around the "Goose Foot" to visit the British, Belgian and French memorials.

◆ The Belgian Monument was erected on the initiative of the veterans to honour their King Albert I because he stayed with them behind the lines for four years. The monument was inaugurated in 1938 at a ceremony attended by Queen Elisabeth and King Leopold III.

The Belgian Monument.

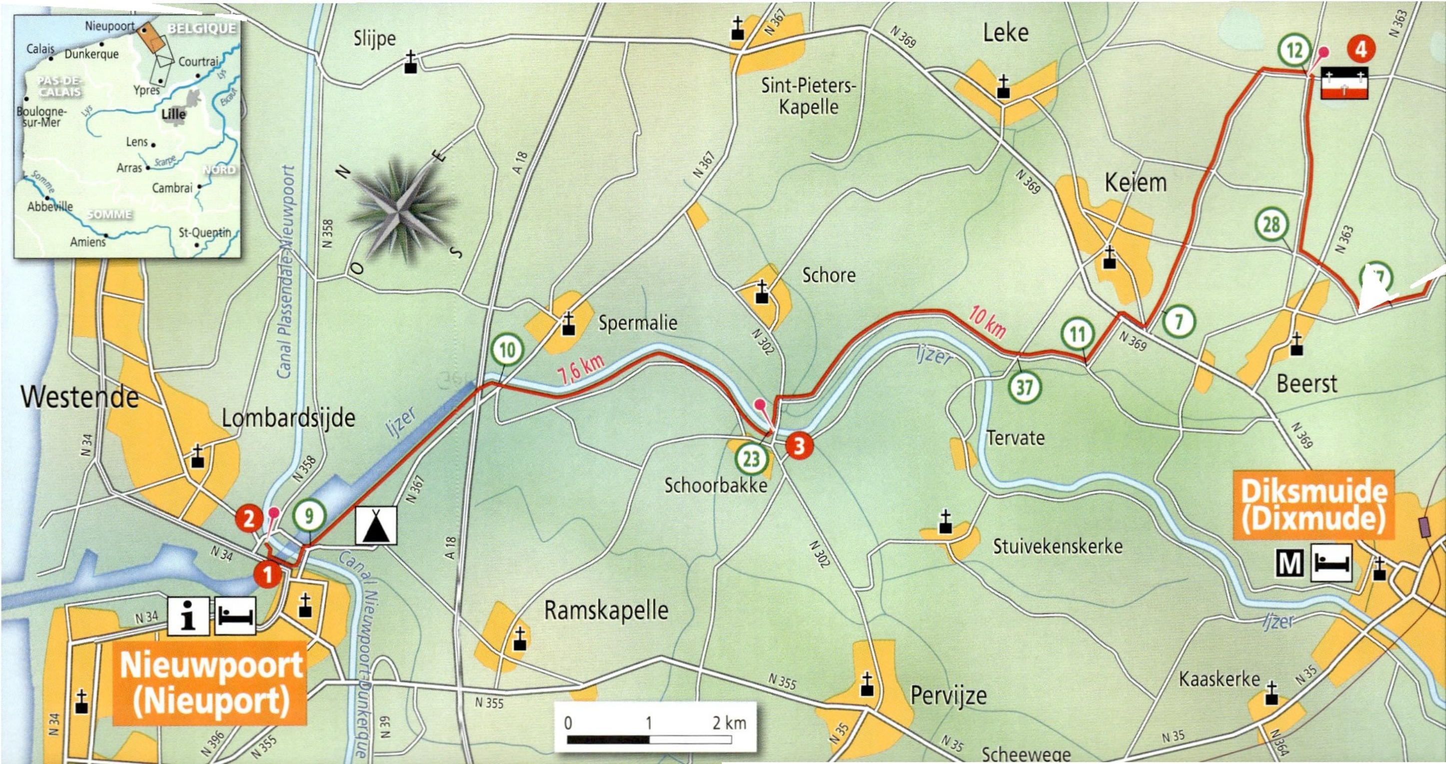

Nieuwpoort
BELGIQUE
Calais
Dunkerque
Courtrai
PAS-DE-CALAIS
Ypres
Boulogne-sur-Mer
Lille
Lens
Arras
NORD
Cambrai
Abbeville
SOMME
St-Quentin
Amiens
Slijpe
Leke
Sint-Pieters-Kapelle
Keiem
Schore
Spermalie
Westende
Lombardsijde
IJzer
Canal Plassendale-Nieuwpoort
Canal Nieuwpoort-Dunkerque
7,6 km
10 km
Tervate
Schoorbakke
Stuivekenskerke
Beerst
Diksmuide (Dixmude)
Ramskapelle
Pervijze
Kaaskerke
Scheewege
Nieuwpoort (Nieuport)
N 34
N 358
N 367
N 369
N 363
N 302
N 355
N 35
N 39
N 396
N 364
A 18
N
E
S
O
0
1
2 km
1
2
3
4
9
10
11
7
12
23
28
37

◆ From the walkway at the top of the gallery the views over the valley of the Yser are impressive. The local clay contained remnants of shrapnel and bullets when it was extracted and fired to make the bricks to build the monument. Today these embedded pieces of metal can still be spotted in the bricks.

3 Follow the semi-circular tour around the "Goose Foot" until you see the cycle lane along the canalised river Yser. Continue 7.5km to the *Schoorbakke* bridge across the Yser. Cross the river and turn right after 350m, then ride straight on for 3.3km up to sign-post 37. Then follow the signs to 11 and 7. Take the N369 for just 260m, then turn left towards 7. From that *knooppunt* you ride straight along *Ramboutstraat* for 3.3km, turning right onto *Houtlandstraat* at the junction.

4 A major German military cemetery is situated just 800m down the road. During the war, 3,233 German soldiers had their final resting place here. In 1956 Belgium closed a number of other German cemeteries around Vladslo, exhumed the remains and buried them all here in this cemetery, bringing the total to 25,644. Peter Kollwitz is one of those buried here. The 1919 Treaty of Versailles allowed the Germans to have one piece of art in their cemeteries.

Die Eltern, The Parents

The sculpture of the grieving parents was produced by artist Käthe Kollwitz. She dedicated this work to her young son, Peter, who fell not far from here on the very day that he arrived at the front. The eyes of the father are fixed on the headstone that bears the name of his son. By evoking the grief caused by the loss of a child, the artist hoped to prevent a similar tragedy from occurring again. Under the Nazis the work of Käthe Kollwitz was considered to be "degenerate" and was banned. Today the statue is an important example of cultural heritage and visitors come from all over the world to admire this work of German expressionism.

Die Eltern, *The Parents.*

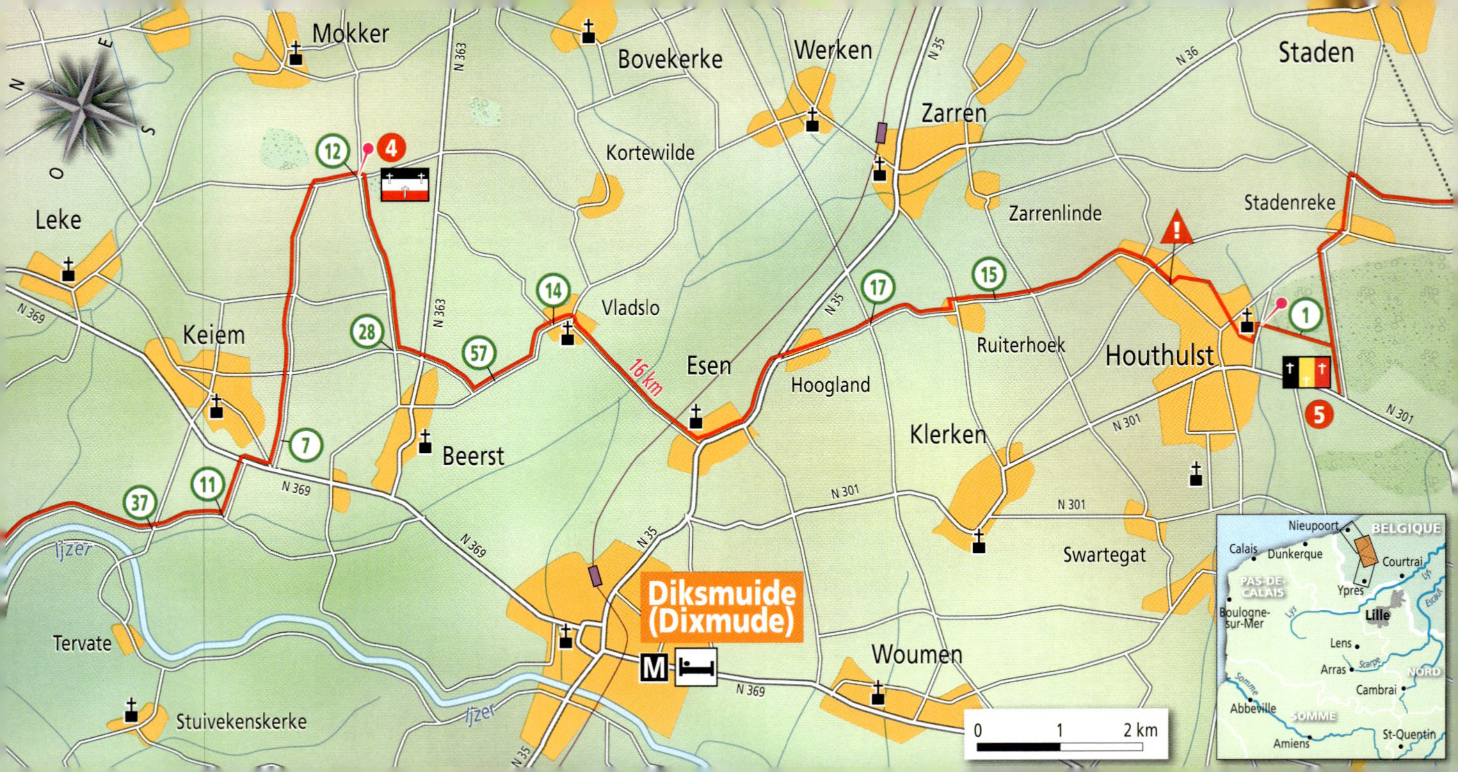

Mokker
Bovekerke
Werken
Zarren
Staden
Kortewilde
Stadenreke
Zarrenlinde
Leke
Vladslo
Keiem
Esen
Hoogland
Ruiterhoek
Houthulst
Klerken
Beerst
Swartegat
Tervate
Diksmuide
(Dixmude)
Woumen
Stuivekenskerke
IJzer
16 km
N 369
N 363
N 35
N 36
N 301
0
1
2 km
Nieuwpoort
BELGIQUE
Calais
Dunkerque
Courtrai
PAS-DE-CALAIS
Ypres
Boulogne-sur-Mer
Lille
Lys
Escaut
Lens
Arras
Scarpe
NORD
Cambrai
Somme
Abbeville
SOMME
Amiens
St-Quentin

◆ Upon leaving the cemetery, turn back to the crossroads at signpost 12, around 400m north of the site. There, turn left and follow the signs for 28 and 57.

◆ Some 5km further on, past post 14 in the village of Vladslo, turn right to the neighbouring village, Esen, around 2.2km further on. Follow the N35 for around 870m before turning into *Veldstraat* on your right.

◆ Pass sign 17 and 2.7km later turn left towards sign 15. Continue straight on for 2.5km along *Terrestraat*, where you will come to a dangerous intersection. The best way to avoid the traffic is to make a left and right turn so that you ride through the residential neighbourhoods of Houthulst.

5 Enter the wood and follow sign 1. In the wood you will find the Belgian military cemetery with 81 Italian tombs.

6 At the opposite end of the wood, towards sign 50, follow an old railway track that is now a cycle path to Langemark, around 6.3km away.

◆ Just before Langemark, turn off the cycle path to visit the second, much larger German military cemetery. Ride on to the church and look for *Korte Ieperstraat*, continuing onto *Cayennestraat*.

The Belgian military cemetery is located in the heart of Houthulst forest and contains the graves of 1,723 Belgian soldiers, most of whom were killed during the «Liberation Offensive» of 1918. 81 Italian soldiers are also buried here.

◆ Cross the fields where the enemy used toxic gas for the first time in this war. At the end of this street, turn left onto the busy N313.

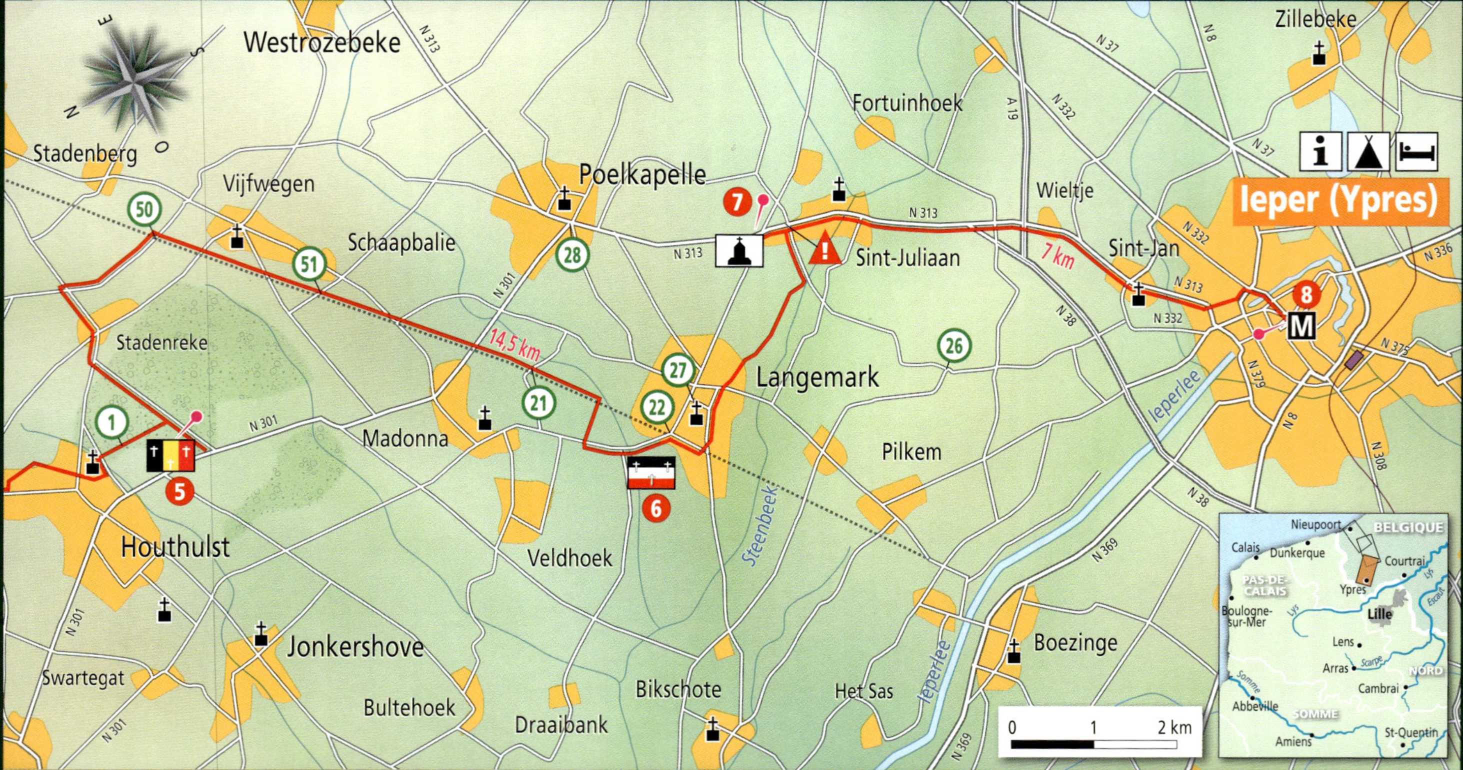
Ieper (Ypres)
Westrozebeke
Stadenberg
Vijfwegen
Schaapbalie
Poelkapelle
Fortuinhoek
Wieltje
Zillebeke
Sint-Juliaan
Sint-Jan
Stadenreke
Langemark
Madonna
Pilkem
Houthulst
Veldhoek
Jonkershove
Swartegat
Bultehoek
Draaibank
Bikschote
Het Sas
Boezinge
Steenbeek
Ieperlee
7 km
14,5 km
N 313
N 301
N 332
N 37
N 8
A 19
N 38
N 369
N 379
N 375
N 308
N 336
0 1 2 km
Nieupoort
BELGIQUE
Calais
Dunkerque
Courtrai
PAS-DE-CALAIS
Ypres
Boulogne-sur-Mer
Lille
Lens
Arras
NORD
Cambrai
Abbeville
SOMME
Amiens
St-Quentin

The "Student" Cemetery

During the First Battle of Ypres, the German commander sent some 9,000 new recruits, students who had left school just a few months earlier, in closed ranks, shoulder to shoulder, onto flat fields with no cover, where they faced a cyclone of British rifle and machine gun fire. The large number of students among the losses caused an emotional shock in the *Heimat*. Years later, Nazi propaganda presented the facts as the slaughter of the innocent youth of the fatherland by brutal British troops. This myth became a significant argument in the German mobilisation in 1939. Hitler personally visited the cemetery on 1 June 1940.

The Studentenfriedhof

British mobilisation

Lord Kitchener, Secretary of State for War and a member of the war cabinet, foresaw a long and brutal war and believed that a only a new force of well-trained and well-led divisions could defeat the Central Powers. Since public opinion was against conscription for foreign wars, Parliament issued a call for volunteers. To persuade men to join, the government launched a campaign which soon featured a distinctive poster of Kitchener. More than two million men answered the call and formed a new national army to be deployed against the enemy on the continent.

The Second Battle of Ypres

To keep this new British army from setting foot on the continent, the Germans planned a second, large-scale offensive to take the Channel ports on the French coast. Since many of their units were engaged in the campaigns in Russia, the enemy needed to bring an element of surprise to confuse the defenders with a secret weapon. No one gave any serious credit to the claims by German prisoners that toxic gas canisters had been hauled to their lines to release gas over Allied lines…

The first use of chemical warfare

On 22 April 1915 the 45th French-African Division was in the first line. It was 5.30pm when the commander was informed that they had been violently attacked by intense artillery fire and that a strange yellow-green cloud was coming from enemy lines. 168 tons of chlorine gas were released over a 6.4km-wide front by the enemy. A thick cloud drifted over the Belgian, French and Canadian lines and quickly filled the trenches, destroying soldiers' lungs and eyes and forcing them to climb out into heavy enemy fire or run for their lives. A 6km (4mile) gap was formed in the front.

The Brooding Soldier

The impressive Canadian Memorial in Saint-Julien stands like a sentinel over the fields where the Canadians had their baptism of fire and bears witness to their heroic stand during the first gas attack of the First World War.

The expression on the face of the soldier, staring over the fields where he lost many of his comrades, his shoulders bowed with folded hands resting on reversed arms, is resolute. In their first appearance on the Western Front the Canadians established a reputation as a formidable fighting force. However the cost was high and offered a grim perspective for future battles.

The Canadians establish a reputation

All through the night, Canadian and assorted French troops manoeuvred to reform a line. The Canadians also mounted a counter-attack to drive the enemy out of Kitchener's Wood. Little ground was gained and casualties were extremely heavy. But these attacks bought precious time to close the flank. On 24 April, the Germans attacked and this time the target was the Canadian line (and the British line on Hill 60). Captain Scrimger, with the 2nd Canadian Field Ambulance, is thought to have passed on the idea to use urine to counteract the gas, and, gasping for air through mud-soaked handkerchiefs, they held on until reinforcements arrived. Ypres was saved.

7 180m further along the N313 stands the Canadian Monument.

8 The road and cycle path along the N313 bring you back to Ypres. 1.2km past the village of Sint-Jan, where the N313 bends to your right, you cross over to the left-hand side of the road and continue straight along *Lindendreef*. Turn left at the end of this street to join the N332 or Menin Road. Ypres was a garrison town where almost every unit of the British imperial forces took a turn to hold the salient lines in front of the town. All marched along the Menin Road to reach their post.

◆ With these first two stages you have cycled 100km, closed the first loop and are ready for the next stage.

The Menin Gate Memorial

Sir Reginald Blomfield was commissioned to design a memorial to commemorate all the Commonwealth soldiers who died in this sector and did not have a known grave. All had marched along the road to Menin, and since the old town gate was no more than a gap in the ramparts, he designed this barrel-vaulted archway. Its large memorial wall contains the names of 54,986 missing soldiers.
On the day of the official opening of the Memorial Gate, the citizens of Ypres wanted to express their gratitude towards those who had given their lives for Belgium's freedom. The local fire brigade came up with the idea of playing the Last Post in the evening; this ceremony has been carried on uninterrupted since 2 July 1928, except for the period when the country was occupied by the Germans during World War II.

Stage 3

From Ypres *(Ieper)* to Armentières

The 1917 Ypres Salient

55km

You leave the town of Ypres by the Menin Gate, just as the soldiers did when they marched to the fields where the Third Battle of Ypres was about to unfold in 1917. After victory at Vimy Ridge (see stage 6) and military success at Messines Ridge (see below), the hope of reclaiming the Belgian ports on the North Sea before the end of the year seemed realistic.

You will discover the beautiful landscapes of the Flemish hills and end this itinerary in the valley of the river Lys, the natural frontier between Belgium and France.

The lion stands guard at the memorial.

The naval campaign and Ypres

In 1917 Germany resumed unrestricted submarine warfare on the Atlantic. With the loss of more than 6,400 ships and 12 million tons of raw materials, the British (war) industry was suffering shortages of all sorts. A new campaign in Flanders aimed to capture the sea bases of the German U-boats on the Belgian coast, Ostend and Zeebrugge. The British commander, Douglas Haig, chose the Ypres Salient for his 1917 operation to secure the Belgian coast and connect with the Dutch border. The Germans controlled the ridges south and east of Ypres. Passchendaele lay on the east ridge of Ypres and it was difficult for the British forces to secure ground observation of the German rear areas east of the ridge.

The Third Battle of Ypres in 1917

In spite of continuous rainfall the plan to attack was maintained. In the north the French divisions were successful and captured Drie Grachten and the area past the canal. Plumer's Second British Army managed to take Hollebeke in the south but in the centre the Germans counter-attacked from behind smokescreens using well-orchestrated artillery fire and mustard gas to drive back the British forces. Further attacks were costly and inconclusive. Haig called a halt to the operations amidst tempestuous weather and General Gough was relieved of his command.

❶ Follow the last 3.5km of the previous (second) stage, so turn left into *Kiplinglaan*, which gives you the best view over the Menin Gate. Once you are on the N313, continue on the cycle path for around 2.5km and turn right immediately after the bridge under the motorway. Ride along *Roeselarestraat* for 4.5km until you are at the white obelisk, where you will turn right.

The New Zealand Division Memorial at 's Graventafel.

Beselare
Keiberg
Zandvoorde
Geluveld
Hollebeke
Molenaarelst
Poezelhoek
Moorslede
Wijtschate
Broodseinde
Tyne Cothoek
Passendale
Zwarte-Leen
Verbrande Molen
Zonnebeke
Zillebeke
St-Elooi
Voormezele
Fortuinhoek
Wieltje
Ieper (Ypres)
Dikkebus Vijver
Dikkebus
Langemark
Sint-Juliaan
Sint-Jan
Ieperlee
10 km
12 km
13 km
0
1
2 km
N 332
N 303
N 8
A 19
N 37
N 336
N 365
N 37b
N 366
N 313
N 38
N 308
Nieuport
BELGIQUE
Calais
Dunkerque
Ypres
Courtrai
PAS-DE-CALAIS
Armentières
Boulogne-sur-Mer
Lille
Lys
Escaut
Lens
Arras
Scarpe
NORD
Cambrai
Somme
Abbeville
SOMME
Amiens
St-Quentin

Second phase: Plumer takes over

Haig transferred authority for the offensive to Plumer, who further developed and fine-tuned the successful tactics introduced by the Canadians on Vimy Ridge (see stage 6). In various stages of well-planned and meticulously executed attacks, each with limited geographical objectives and accurate short- to medium-range artillery barrages, he secured success on the Menin Road (20 September), at Polygon Wood (26 September) and at Broodseinde (4 October). It was during this stage that the ANZAC Divisions made a successful advance and arrived at the foot of Passchendaele.

❷ The obelisk is a memorial to the New Zealand Division in the salient. As you ride along *Shipstraat* you see in the distance the largest Commonwealth military cemetery in the world. Turn left after 1.3km and you will arrive at the gate of Tyne Cot Cemetery, a silent witness of the horror that took place here in 1917. There are toilets in the car park and a path leading to the visitor centre.

The Tyne Cot Memorial to the Missing.

The King's Pilgrimage

In the centre you will see a big German pillbox; after it was captured, it served as a field dressing station for the Commonwealth troops in October 1917. When King George V visited this cemetery in 1922 he suggested that the Cross of Sacrifice should be erected on top of this German pillbox and that the 343 soldiers who had been buried around it by their comrades should not be exhumed and reburied; their graves therefore remain in an irregular layout, unlike the rest of the post-war cemetery with its straight rows and evenly spaced headstones.

The Battle of Passchendaele

The first assault on Passchendaele was not properly planned, and just 48 hours after the four ANZAC Divisions went over the top to storm Passchendaele they had ceased to exist as a combat force. Tyne Cot Cemetery contains the graves of 1,353 Australian soldiers. In late October the four Canadian divisions resumed the attack and after three weeks of bitter fighting and 16,000 casualties they finally reached the village. The last geographical obstacle between Ypres and the Belgian coast was won and hopes were revived that the Allies would be able to push through to the ports. An early winter, however, covered the roads with snow and made any transport of men and supplies impossible. The offensive came to a definitive stop.

The Canadian Memorial Stone.

3 Upon leaving the car park, turn left and ride towards Passendale (the modern name for Passchendaele) on a country road that runs parallel to the N303. After 1.7km, turn left into *Martinegatstraat*, which takes you to the Canadian memorial site.

4 *Canadalaan* (Canada Street) leads to the rebuilt church; turn right onto the N303 and after 950m you trade the concrete road for an old railway track, now an asphalt cycle path that cuts through the fields all the way to the village of Zonnebeke with its Art Deco church.

◆ The public park behind the church is perfect for a moment of relaxation, and nearby you will also find the Passchendaele Museum (www.passchendaele.be). The unique feature of this museum is a replica of a 33ft-deep dugout and a presentation of the "underground war" in Flanders. Leave the park via the car park, turn onto *Berten Pilstraat* and

Polygon Wood

Before the war the Belgian officers used a track in this wood to train their horses, and in the centre a large mound, known as the *Butte*, was used for rifle practice. Under German occupation this *Butte* became a defensive stronghold with underground shelters and concrete machine gun posts. In September 1917 this was the hardest nut to crack and this mission was given to the 5th Australian. In a well-planned and well-executed battle the artillery laid a carpet of bombs in front of the advancing infantrymen and this position was captured in one day. The 5th Australian Division Memorial on the *Butte* testifies to this glorious victory by the 5th Division, which somewhat compensated for the tragedy of Fromelles (see stage 5).

Five headstones were inaugurated on 26 September 2007 and the men were re-buried with full honours, 90 years after the battle.

The plaque for the 5th Australian Division.

ride uphill to the first junction, where you turn right into *Grote Molenstraat*, then immediately left into *Citernestraat* towards Polygon Wood, which can be seen in the distance.

◆ The remains of five Australian Imperial Force (AIF) soldiers were discovered by chance in September 2006 during road works. Subsequent DNA testing enabled three of the five men to be identified.

❺ Your route goes around the wood, where you cross the A19 motorway. *Kabouterstraat* takes you straight to the N8 or Menin Road. Ride downhill for 1.8km and turn left at the sign for Hill 62, where there is a local trench museum that is worth a visit. At the roundabout where the road ends you can walk up the hill and enjoy the spectacular view.

FRANCE
BELGIQUE
NORD
IEPER
Armentières
Frelinghien
Houplines
Warneton
Hollebeke
Gapaard
Oosttaverne
Verbrande Molen
Mesen
Le Bizet
Wijtschate
St-Elooi
Voormezele
Le Rossignol
Ploegsteert
Vierstraat
Wulvergem
Nieuwkerke
Kemmel
Nieppe
la Lys
La Deûle
La Lys
Douvebeek
D 108
D 949
D 945
N 58A
N 314
N 58
N 336
N 365
N 331
N 515
D 422
D 933
A 25
12 km
7,5 km
4,5 km
5 km
0
1
2 km
Nieuport
Calais
Dunkerque
Ypres
Courtrai
PAS-DE-CALAIS
Armentières
Lille
Boulogne-sur-Mer
Lens
Arras
Cambrai
Abbeville
SOMME
Amiens
St-Quentin
NORD
Somme
Scarpe
Escaut
Lys

6 The signpost at the roundabout indicates a short gravel road to *Pappotstraat*, which leads straight onto *Werviksestraat*, where you turn right and follow the signs for Hill 60.

◆ This hill is situated 4.5km from the market square in Ypres, and its elevated position made it a strategic observation point that was coveted by both sides. With the trenches just 40 yards away, it was a sector that saw fierce fighting – every soldier knew and feared this position. After the war a chaplain bought this patch of land to preserve the ground as it was left after the battles. The craters testify to the 1916 and 1917 tunnelling and mining operations (see below, The Battle of Messines).

7 From Hill 59, continue to the end of this road, and 2.4km further along the cycle path beside *Komenseweg* you will arrive in Hollebeke. Turn right into *Hollebekestraat*. Follow signs 51 and then 50 to Wijtschate Square, where you turn onto the road to Kemmel. After 1.5km, turn at the sign for Spanbroekmolen, another crater. The wooden gate in the enclosure and the stone path lead to a pretty pond. As you leave the site, the panoramic view with two slag heaps and Vimy Ridge on the horizon illustrate the strategic importance this position held during the war.

"Lone Tree Crater".

The Celtic cross adjacent to the military cemetery commemorates the 16th Division. You will find an identical cross in Guillemont, in the Somme (Special Outing 3).

Messines Ridge

Known as the crest of Flanders, Messines Ridge is the high ground south of Ypres that offered a view over the Allied defences. It was a thorn in the side of the British commanders that the Germans could monitor their build-up of troops and preparations and could control the rear areas from which the British intended to conduct the advance to Passchendaele and the Belgian coast in 1917. Lieutenant-General Herbert Plumer recommended to Field Marshal Sir Douglas Haig that Messines Ridge be captured before attempting an operation further north.

The Battle of Messines Ridge

Improved maps, new sound-ranging equipment and better communications made the counter-artillery increasingly effective in suppressing the German artillery. Tunnelling had begun in 1916 and miners were instructed to lay 22 mines with 450 tons of ammonal explosives. Early in the morning on 7 June, 19 mines exploded and the artillery fired a creeping barrage immediately ahead of the nine advancing infantry divisions that went over the top in a steady pace behind the barrage. By 2:00pm the set objectives had been taken in what is considered to be a model battle and described as a tactical and operational success.

8 From the crater you ride downhill towards Messines, but turn right after 1km onto *Menenstraat* and right again down *Kortestraat*, which leads to the N314. To continue to New Zealand Street, you first have to turn right and ride for

The Irish Peace Park.

150m to the junction, where you leave the busy road for a gentle climb towards Messines. Just before the edge of the towpath is New Zealand Park with an obelisk identical to the one we saw previously at 's Graventafel. The New Zealand Division fulfilled its mission brilliantly by taking the church.

A simple wooden cross to commemorate the Christmas Truce.

The consequences of the spontaneous truce

This fraternisation with the enemy went on for a couple more days. The news could not be reported by the press in Belgium, France or Germany, but a picture of the British playing the Germans found its way to the British newspapers; word had got out and the story spread around the world. The military considered any form of fraternisation with the enemy as treason that needed to be swept under the carpet. The fact that the soldiers had refused to fight once the officers had gone home to be with their families was embarrassing. The commanders learned their lesson, and in 1915 the officers stayed with the troops to avoid any possibility of a repeat performance.

◆ The 4.5km cycle path on the N365 from Messines to Ploegsteert (named "Plug Street" by the soldiers) passes the Irish Peace Park and the valley of the Douve and climbs Hill 63 before reaching the flat valley of the Lys.

◆ If there is enough energy left in your legs and you feel like hearing one of the heart-warming stories of the war, turn left at the sign "Bairnsfather plaque" just before the top of Hill 63. This leads to the spot where both sides played a game of football on Christmas Day 1914.

The Ploegsteert Memorial.

9 You can either ride back to the N365 to reach the Ploegsteert Memorial or take a shortcut by following the sign for Mud Corner Cemetery and staying on the gravel path until you see the memorial. Since 7 June 1999, the *Comité du Memorial de Ploegsteert* has arranged for the Last Post to be played at the memorial on the first Friday of each month. The *Auberge* where Nelly and Claude serve drinks and food is a great place to take a break.

◆ At the roundabout, go around the little square, and at the steps to the entrance of the old town hall you will find a plaque.

One of the lions stands guard and one is bearing his teeth in warning

⑩ After riding for 1.5km you will be happy to leave the N365. The *Chemin de la Blanche* and *Drèves des Rabecques* will take you to the river Lys, the natural border between Belgium and France. Around a hundred yards before you cross the bridge you will see the sign for a farmhouse and B&B, which can become very busy at weekends but is a haven of peace during the week and a great place to discover (www.lahowarderie.be).

◆ The bridge across the Lys and towpath along the river take you to the town of Armentières, the starting point for stages 4 and 5 and linked to the city of Lille by Special Outing 1.

Winston Churchill

After he resigned as First Lord of the Admiralty, Winston Churchill served as Commanding Officer (Lieutenant-Colonel) of the 6th Battalion of the Royal Scots Fusiliers here from January to May 1916. His experience of German defences made him an advocate of the plan to build an armoured "land ship" on tracks with the ability to cut through entangled wires and span a five-foot trench. The Royal Navy played a decisive role in the development and production of this plan. Its codename, given because the shape of the shell resembled a water carrier, was "tank"; the name stuck.

A local artist depicts Churchill as we remember him from WWII in WWI clothing – we'll put it down to artistic licence!

Stage 4

From Armentières to Ypres *(Ieper)*

Hospitals and casualty clearing stations behind Allied lines

47km

This stage includes quiet country roads and gentle climbs on the hills along the French-Belgian border. Stages 3 and 4 combined make a 100km loop with plenty of history.

The large hospital cemeteries tell a different aspect of the conflict that opposed empires. 12km (9 miles) behind the lines, medical staff performed miracles the save the men whom the military had tried so hard to kill. You will discover the story of two of these heroes who were committed to saving lives.

The banks of the river Lys.

❶ In front of the town hall, in *Place du Général de Gaulle*, you will find the obelisk and statue of the French soldier, originally with the defeated German eagle under his foot. During the Second World War the Germans found this detail offensive and had the eagle removed, and today we see just a chunk of stone and the vague outline of the eagles' wings.

Armentières, the hospital town behind the lines

In October 1914, British units controlled Armentières and established a continuous line from Ypres to La Basée (see stage 5) on the Canal d'Aire. Armentières was just far enough behind the battle zone to have a permanent military base with hospitals for the care and treatment of thousands of wounded soldiers during the war.

During the second phase of the German offensive in Flanders in spring 1918, known as the Battle of the Lys, the enemy captured and occupied Armentières until 2 October and made use of the British hospitals and cemeteries.

◆ The town hall and Belfry had to be completely rebuilt after the war. The distinctive red brick architecture was the work of Louis-Marie Cordonnier, who designed most of the official buildings in this area.

◆ Behind the hall is the church, where you make your way to the towpath along the river towards the bridges and the D933 to Bailleul.

◆ 300m after the bridge you can ride parallel to the busy D933 along the following streets: *Rue de Gand* and *Rue Gambetta*.

Armentières Town Hall.

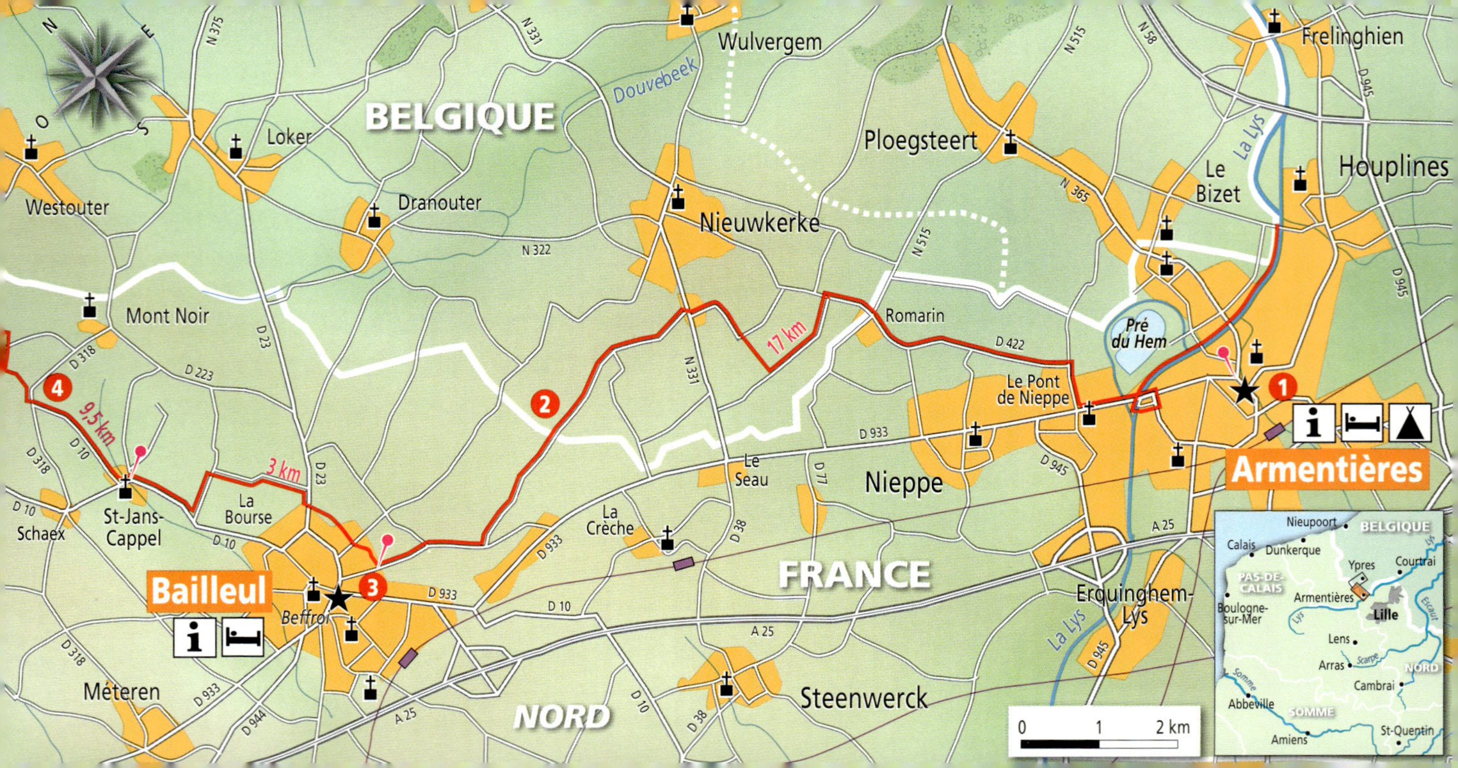

BELGIQUE
FRANCE
NORD
Armentières
Bailleul
Beffroi
Frelinghien
Houplines
Le Bizet
Ploegsteert
Wulvergem
Nieuwkerke
Dranouter
Loker
Westouter
Mont Noir
Romarin
Pré du Hem
Le Pont de Nieppe
Nieppe
Le Seau
La Crèche
Erquinghem-Lys
Steenwerck
La Bourse
St-Jans-Cappel
Schaex
Méteren
Douvebeek
La Lys
17 km
3 km
9,5 km
1
2
3
4
N 375
N 331
N 58
N 515
N 365
N 322
D 945
D 422
D 933
D 77
D 38
D 23
D 223
D 318
D 10
D 944
A 25
0
1
2 km
Nieupoort
Calais
Dunkerque
Ypres
Courtrai
PAS-DE-CALAIS
Armentières
Lille
Boulogne-sur-Mer
Lens
Arras
Scarpe
Escaut
NORD
Cambrai
Somme
Abbeville
SOMME
Amiens
St-Quentin

The French Soldier.

❷ *Rue du Pavé Fruit* and then *Rue du Pontceau* to leave Armentières and Nieppe behind you and follow the D422 from France into Belgium. 650m after crossing the border, turn into *Groenestraat* on your left, then *Potteriestraat*. Join the N331 briefly before turning onto *Eikelstraat*. At the French border, turn left onto the street named *Eeckelstraete* to reach the military cemetery.

❸ Bailleul Communal Cemetery contains 4,403 Commonwealth graves from the First World War. There are also 17 Commonwealth graves from the Second World War and 154 German graves from both wars. You don't visit Bailleul itself but leave via the D23 and after 700m turn left into *Callyn Straete*. After 1.5km it is better to turn left and continue on the D10.

◆ If you happen to be riding a mountain bike or the weather's dry you may continue on the non-asphalted part of the same track. 200m after Saint-Jans-Cappel church, turn right into *Rue Chieux*, which leads to the D318. Follow this road for 240m.

The Mademoiselles from Armentières

After the ANZAC soldiers evacuated Gallipoli and left Egypt for France in 1916, this became their sector. Since they could not return home for the usual short period of rest and recuperation every six weeks, the "French Mademoiselles" offered an attractive alternative when they had time and money to spend in Armentières. One of the most popular wartime songs is Mademoiselle from Armentieres, also known by its ersatz French line Hinky Dinky Parlez-vous (or Parley voo). It was considered a risqué song, and poked fun at the officers for not being anywhere near the front line, instead spending their time with French ladies… The tune was resurrected again during the Second World War.

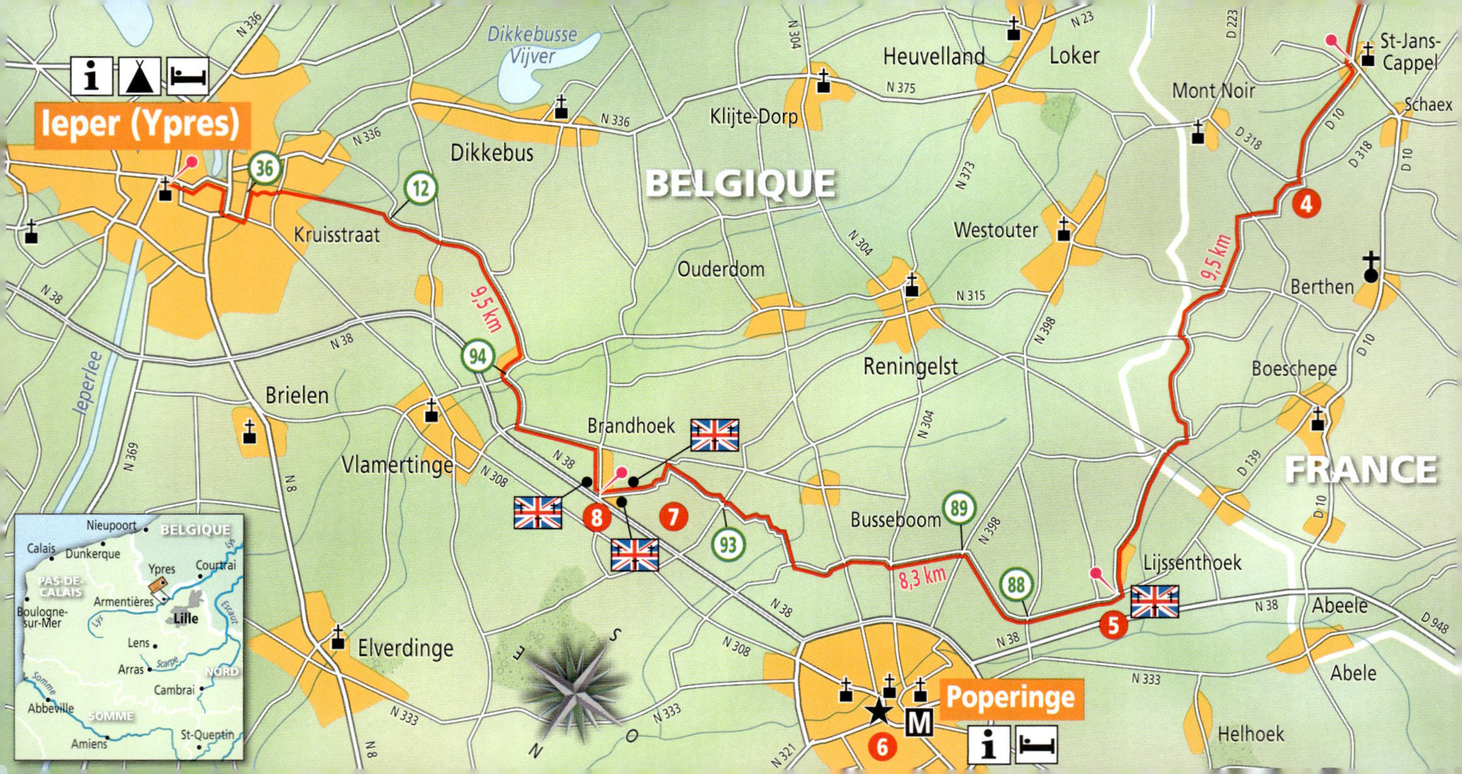
Ieper (Ypres)
Dikkebusse Vijver
Dikkebus
Kruisstraat
BELGIQUE
Heuvelland
Loker
Klijte-Dorp
Mont Noir
St-Jans-Cappel
Schaex
Westouter
Ouderdom
Berthen
Reningelst
Boeschepe
Brielen
Brandhoek
Vlamertinge
FRANCE
Busseboom
Lijssenthoek
Abeele
Abele
Elverdinge
Poperinge
Helhoek
Ieperlee
9,5 km
9,5 km
8,3 km
N 336
N 38
N 369
N 8
N 308
N 333
N 321
N 304
N 375
N 373
N 315
N 398
N 23
D 223
D 318
D 10
D 139
D 948
12
36
94
93
89
88
4
5
6
7
8
S
O
N
E
Nieuport
BELGIQUE
Calais
Dunkerque
Ypres
Courtrai
PAS-DE-CALAIS
Boulogne-sur-Mer
Armentières
Lille
Lys
Escaut
Lens
Arras
Scarpe
NORD
Cambrai
Somme
Abbeville
SOMME
Amiens
St-Quentin

The large military cemetery mostly contains the graves of soldiers from the Commonwealth.

There is a plot with crosses for French soldiers, but you will also find Chinese and other nationalities.

Exploring the cemetery before you enter the visitor centre helps give you an idea of the sheer scale of the place.

4 Halfway up the climb to the top of *Mont Noir* you take the little road on your left, *Chemin de la Levrette*, and 800m further *Rue du Pudefort*, which you follow all the way to the end. There you go right and a little further turn left onto *Rue Coustenoble*. At the end of that street you can't go straight on, so turn left and immediately right onto the winding *Rue des Sept Mesures*. At the T-junction turn right into *Petit Chemin de Poperinghe*.

The most frequently visited headstone is one of a woman, Nellie Spindler. She worked as a staff nurse at Brandhoek casualty clearing station (or CCS, see below). She died of her injuries shortly after her post was shelled. Her grave reference is plot 16, row A, headstone 3.

Leland Wingate Fernald was an American volunteer who enlisted to avenge the sinking of the Lusitania, as we read on the epitaph on his grave. His grave reference is plot 6, row C, headstone 36a.

❺ You cross borders one more time and 2km further on you come to Lijssenthoek Military Cemetery, the largest hospital cemetery with more than 10,700 graves.

❻ To continue the route, follow signpost 89. The return to Ypres follows more or less the same route that the ambulances drove to and from the front with an inevitable stop at Brandhoek CCS. To see Poperinge and visit Talbot House, a unique stopping point on your journey, follow sign 92.

◆ Just like Armentières, Poperinge or "Pops" was a place behind the lines where the men could find all sorts of entertainment. A priest and a padre decided to open an alternative place to find rest and spiritual comfort in a haven of peace where there was no need to justify one's presence or how long one wished to simply sit and brood. On 11 December 1915, the house at 43 Gasthuisstraat (at that time the street was known by its French name, Rue de l'Hôpital) opened its doors for the first time, welcoming British soldiers to a new club. This house with very few rules became a pilgrimage place for veterans after the war when they returned to commemorate their lost pals.

Talbot House. (www.talbothouse.be)

❼ The route to Ypres follows sign 93. One cemetery is situated a little outside that signposted route so you should return to sign 93 after your visit.

❽ Four military cemeteries testify that this CCS was an important medical centre and hub 5km behind the front. For many this was the end of their journey. The remarkable captain Noel Chavasse, a doctor in the Royal Army Medical Corps, died of his wounds here and is buried at Brandhoek New Military Cemetery (grave ref.: plot 3, row B, headstone 15).

◆ Turn left upon leaving the cemetery and then turn right 160m further on to return to the signposted itinerary to Ypres. Signs 94, 12 and 36 will take you straight back to the town.

Captain Noel Godfrey Chavasse

Noel Godfrey Chavasse was first awarded the Victoria Cross in 1916 for his actions in Guillemont, France (see Special Outing 3), where he rescued and attended to men in no man's land all day under heavy fire. It is said he got as close as 25 yards to the German line, where he found three men, and continued throughout the night under a constant rain of sniper bullets and bombing. In 1917 during the offensive at Passchendaele he 'performed his duties for two days and went out repeatedly under enemy fire to search and attend to the wounded who were lying out'. During these searches he was injured and died of his wounds. He was awarded a second VC to become the most highly decorated British serviceman in the war.

His military headstone carries, uniquely, a representation of two Victoria Crosses.

***Special Outing* 1**

From Armentières to Lille

Occupation and resistance

27km

The city of Lille, situated on the river Deûle, became French under Louis XIV. Today it is the capital of the French department Nord and trains from all over the continent converge here, making the "capital of the north" an important crossroads.

This outing links your itinerary on the old Western Front to the fourth largest city in France and its gateway to the UK, Eurostar.

The towpath along the river Lys leads to the confluence with the Deûle where you again follow the towpath all the way to the citadel in Lille.

The towpath on the river Deûle.

❶ Riding along the river banks from Armentières to Lille is a comfortable, flat journey where you hardly leave the towpath. At the sluices (*écluses*) you cross the waterway on the yellow drawbridge.

◆ When the King of France, Louis XIV, took the city from the Spanish he ordered the construction of a citadel to control and defend it. The plan by famous French architect Vauban was chosen and today it is one of the most impressive relics of that type of military fortification in terms of both its size and its excellent state of preservation.

The drawbridge.

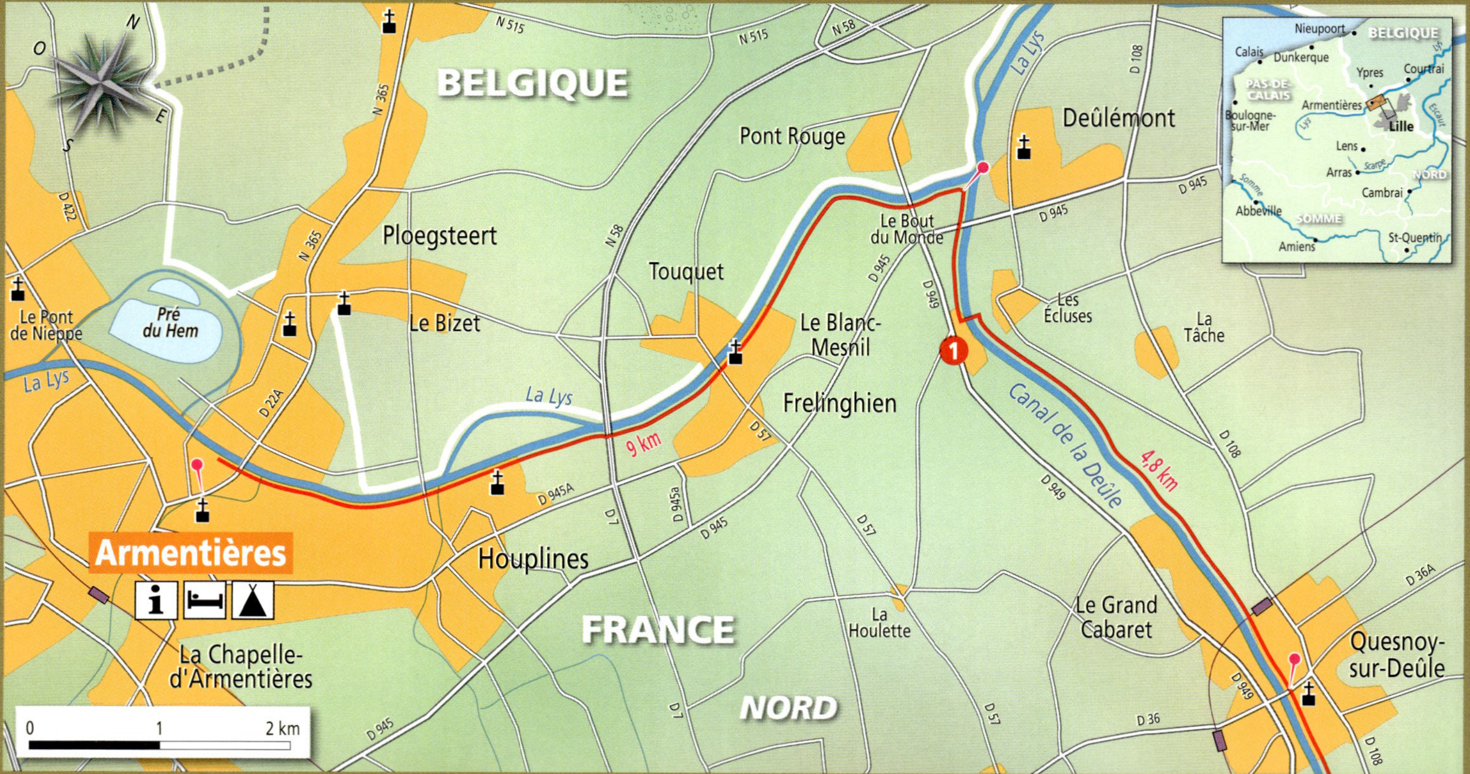
BELGIQUE
FRANCE
NORD
Armentières
Houplines
La Chapelle-
d'Armentières
Le Pont
de Nieppe
Pré
du Hem
Ploegsteert
Le Bizet
Touquet
Pont Rouge
Le Blanc-
Mesnil
Frelinghien
Le Bout
du Monde
Deûlémont
Les
Écluses
La
Tâche
La
Houlette
Le Grand
Cabaret
Quesnoy-
sur-Deûle
La Lys
Canal de la Deûle
9 km
4,8 km
N 515
N 58
N 365
D 422
D 22A
D 945A
D 945a
D 945
D 949
D 7
D 57
D 108
D 36
D 36A
0
1
2 km
Nieupoort
Calais
Dunkerque
Ypres
Courtrai
Boulogne-
sur-Mer
Armentières
Lille
Lens
Arras
Cambrai
Abbeville
Amiens
St-Quentin
PAS-DE-
CALAIS
SOMME

◆ Modern Lille is the main city of Lille Métropole, the fourth-largest metropolitan area in France after Paris, Lyon and Marseille. Lille is situated on the Deûle River, near France's border with Belgium. It is the capital of the Nord-Pas de Calais region and the prefecture of the Nord department.

◆ In 1914 the Germans occupied Lille to install their *Kommandantur* (headquarters) and several military hospitals there. The opera house was renamed the German Theatre. The Germans organised a system to requisition raw materials and labour forces from the city and the surrounding countryside. Civilian prisoners were used as human shields and hostages.

To prevent espionage from developing, the Germans introduced brutal repressive measures. More than 21 public executions took place.

One of the victims was a young Belgian student, Léon Trulin, who had been rejected by the Belgian army because he was too young. He turned to the British, who recruited and trained him to gather intelligence He was only 18 years old when he was executed at the ramparts of the citadel on 8 November 1915.

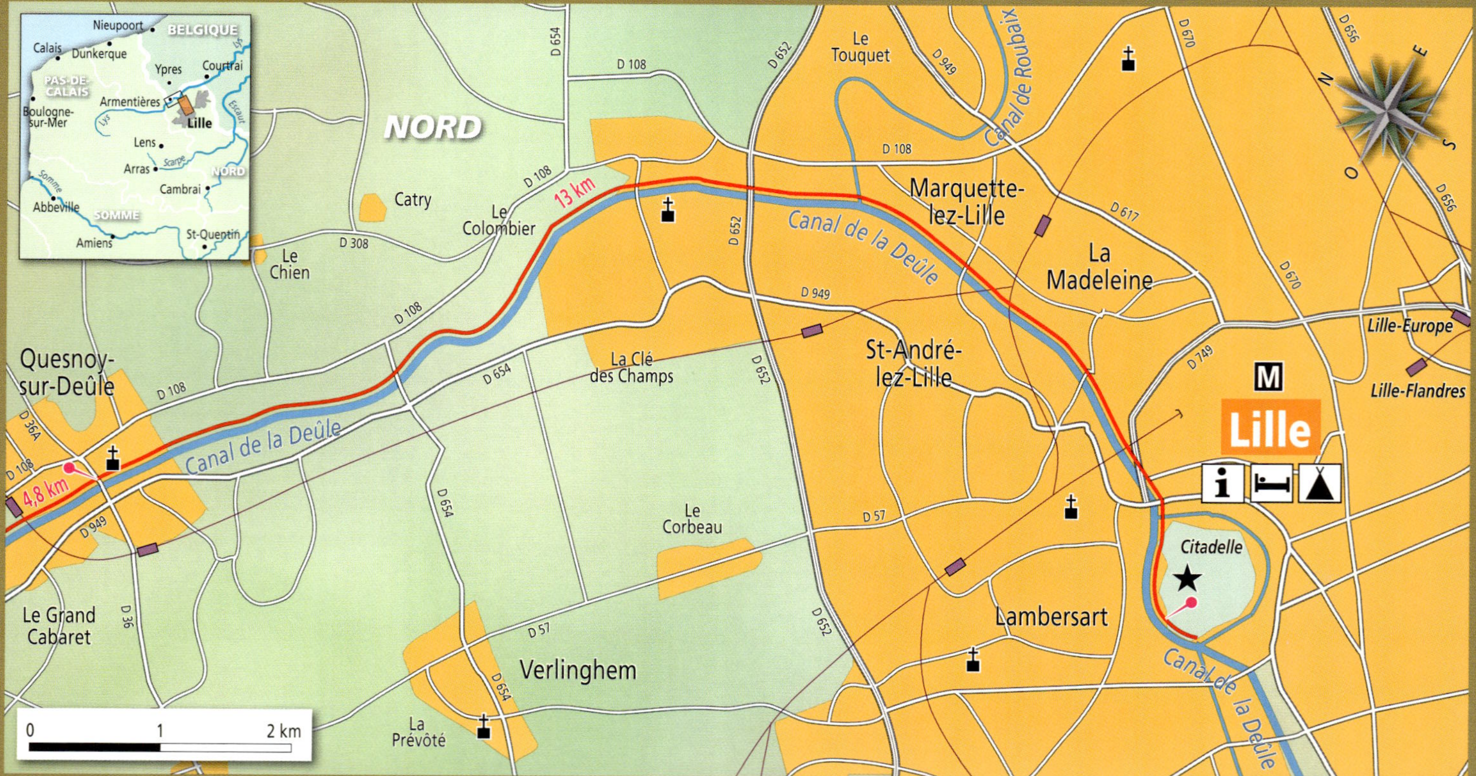

Nieuport
BELGIQUE
Calais
Dunkerque
Ypres
Courtrai
PAS-DE-CALAIS
Armentières
Boulogne-sur-Mer
Lille
Lens
Arras
NORD
Cambrai
Abbeville
SOMME
St-Quentin
Amiens
Lys
Escaut
Scarpe
Somme
NORD
Catry
Le Colombier
13 km
Le Chien
Quesnoy-sur-Deûle
4,8 km
Le Grand Cabaret
Canal de la Deûle
La Clé des Champs
Le Corbeau
Verlinghem
La Prévôté
Le Touquet
Canal de Roubaix
Marquette-lez-Lille
La Madeleine
St-André-lez-Lille
Lambersart
Lille
M
Citadelle
Lille-Europe
Lille-Flandres
D 654
D 108
D 652
D 308
D 36A
D 949
D 36
D 57
D 617
D 670
D 656
D 749
N
E
S
O
0
1
2 km

The "Alice" network

Louise de Bettignies was a modern young woman who was fluent in French, English and German. She was recruited and trained by the Allied intelligence services to work behind the lines in the occupied zone to gather intelligence for the Allies.
She took the codename of Alice Dubois and ran a vast network in northern France and Belgium. More than 80 people watched trains, followed the movements of artillery units, mapped ammunition depots and enemy communication and commandment centres and provided valuable information. She also assisted Allied soldiers to fly to the Netherlands, which had remained neutral.

The Queen of Spies

Louise fell into a trap and was arrested and sentenced to death by the German military council in Brussels. Edith Cavell had been executed shortly before her and the international outcry made the Germans convert Louise's sentence into forced labour. After being held for three years, she died on 27 September 1918 as a result of complications during an operation on a pleural abscess and was buried under a simple wooden cross (see stage 7) in Westfriedhof.
After the war her remains were repatriated and on 16 March 1920 a funeral was held in Lille with full military honours. Her body is buried in the cemetery of Saint-Amand-les-Eaux.

Louise de Bettignies.

Stage 5
From Armentières to Lens
The coal-mining area in the Douai Plains

46km

This stage, rich in history, makes the link between Flanders and Artois and also between Flanders and the Somme. Although the lines hardly moved in this sector over the four years, it was certainly not for want of attacks and offensives. Many memorials commemorate the battles that took place here in 1915 and 1916. This route passes through the Douai Plains, the most industrialised part of France in the 20th century. In 2013 the famous French museum the Louvre opened a subsidiary on a former mine site.

The plains and spoil heaps of Douai.

❶ From Armentières main square take *Rue du Maréchal Foch*, turn left and then head down *Rue Sadi Carnot* for 1km. *Rue d'Erquinghem* brings you to the D945. Before crossing the railway and leaving Armentières behind you, visit the Cité Bonjean Military Cemetery, an interesting addition to stage 4. The school in *Avenue Salengro* was the site of a large military hospital that treated casualties from a wide sector south of Ypres to Lille.

◆ In the German spring offensive of 1918 the city was lost to the Germans, who occupied it for six months, using the existing facilities and burying their soldiers in a row adjacent to the Commonwealth burials.

It is unusual to see the headstones of German and Commonwealth soldiers side by side.

Aubers Ridge in 1915

The German belt of defence around Lille was situated some 20km outside the city. The British knew the sector as Aubers Ridge, named after the larger of the two villages on the high ground. In order to support the French attacks north of Arras (see stage 6), the British forces launched two subsidiary attacks here. The duration and the weight of the artillery bombardment were wholly insufficient to break the German wire and breastwork defences. This battle was an unmitigated disaster for the British army. No ground was won and no tactical advantage gained. English, Scottish and Indian units together suffered more than 11,000 casualties.

❷ 1.8km further along the D945, just past the town hall of Erquinghem, turn left into *Rue Delpierre* and continue to Fleurbaix. Be careful on the D171 in Fleurbaix. The first street on your left, *Rue des Crombions,* is a good place to leave the D171 and find quiet roads in totally flat farming country. Turn right at the end of the road onto *Rue des Lombards* and you will see two military cemeteries in *Rue du Petillon* or the D175. The D22C leads you to Fromelles.

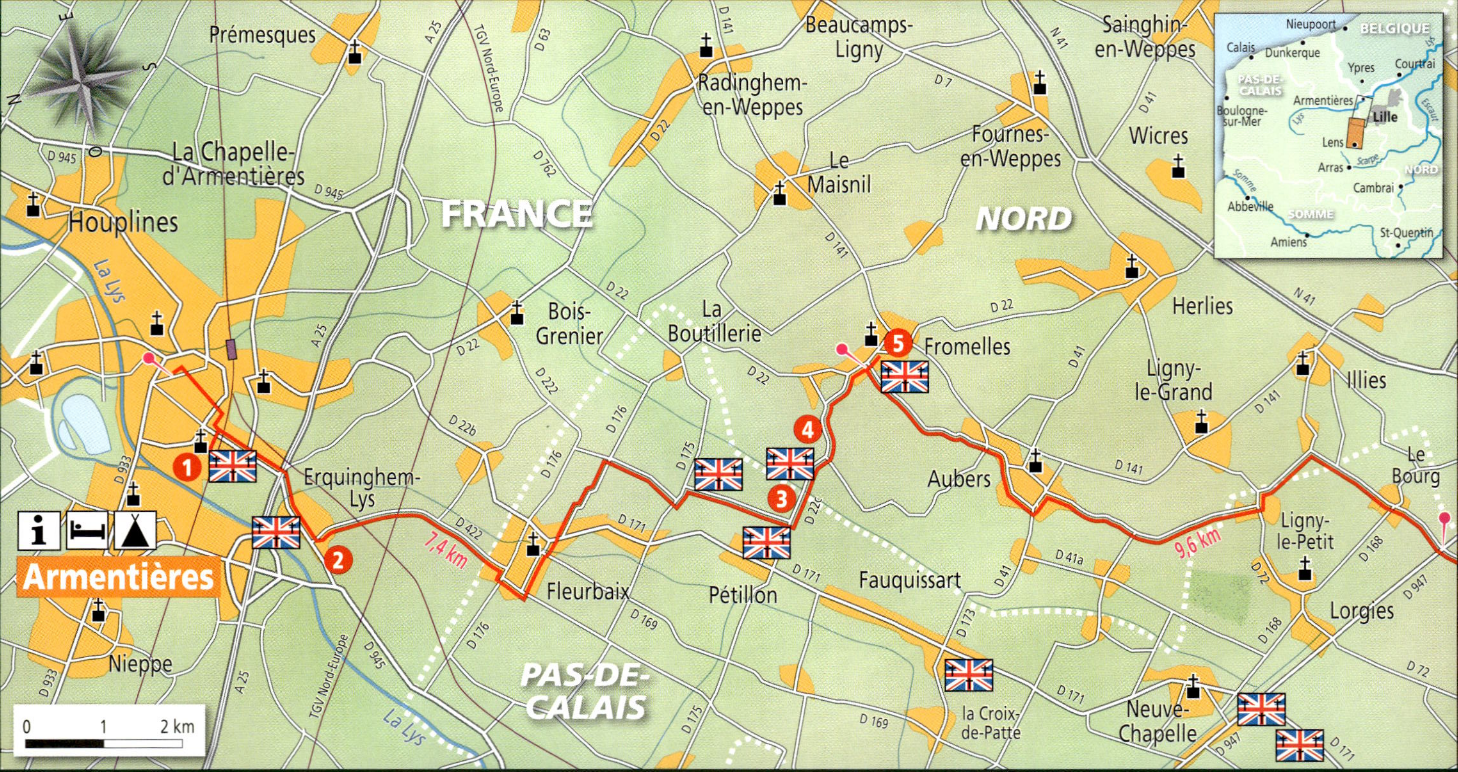

Armentières
Houplines
La Chapelle-d'Armentières
Prémesques
Nieppe
La Lys
Erquinghem-Lys
FRANCE
NORD
PAS-DE-CALAIS
Bois-Grenier
La Boutillerie
Radinghem-en-Weppes
Beaucamps-Ligny
Le Maisnil
Fournes-en-Weppes
Wicres
Sainghin-en-Weppes
Herlies
Fromelles
Ligny-le-Grand
Illies
Aubers
Le Bourg
Ligny-le-Petit
Lorgies
Fleurbaix
Pétillon
Fauquissart
la Croix-de-Patte
Neuve-Chapelle
7,4 km
9,6 km
1
2
3
4
5
TGV Nord-Europe
A 25
D 945
D 933
D 63
D 762
D 22
D 22b
D 222
D 422
D 176
D 175
D 171
D 169
D 141
D 7
D 41
D 41a
N 41
D 173
D 72
D 168
D 947
0
1
2 km
Nieuport
BELGIQUE
Calais
Dunkerque
Ypres
Courtrai
PAS-DE-CALAIS
Armentières
Lille
Boulogne-sur-Mer
Lens
Arras
NORD
Cambrai
Abbeville
SOMME
Somme
Amiens
St-Quentin
Lys
Scarpe
Escaut

A diversion turns into a massacre in 1916

Two freshly formed divisions were too inexperienced to be engaged in the Somme and were ordered to fake an attack so that German reserves would be tied down here rather than being sent to the Somme. The training of these two divisions was carried out in full view of the Germans, who hauled all their reserves and were armed and ready to defend their positions. When the local British commander became greedy and ordered the two divisions to charge the opponent in broad daylight in open flat fields with no cover, the men were decimated. In less than 48 hours the 5th Australian Division lost half of its men in its first taste of action on the Western Front.

V.C. Corner Cemetery and Memorial.

◆ Given the flat topography, an 8m-high rise in the fields makes a strategic vantage point. This 2-3km area of slightly higher ground contains the villages of Aubers and Fromelles. Because Aubers is the bigger village of the two, the rise is known as Aubers Ridge.

❸ V.C. Corner Cemetery was created after the end of the war and contains the graves of 410 Australian soldiers who were killed during the Battle of Fromelles and whose bodies were found on the battlefield. As none of the bodies could be identified, it was decided to record on a memorial all the names of Australian soldiers who were killed in the offensive and whose graves were never found.

Mass graves in Pheasant Wood

The battle left 8,000 dead and badly wounded who were crying out for help in no man's land. A truce was offered by the German commander to give time to search and bring in the wounded and return the Allied bodies that lay on German-held ground, but it was turned down by the British commander, Haking, who moreover gave strict orders not to leave the trenches at night to search. The Germans had to bury the bodies of both their own and Commonwealth soldiers who were interred in five pits in Pheasant Wood. In 2009 these were exhumed to be reburied in a Commonwealth military cemetery.

Simon Fraser.

4 The bravery of those who went out to rescue the wounded of Fromelles is commemorated at the Australian Memorial Park. In the centre of the Memorial Park we see the statue of Simon Fraser carrying a wounded man on his shoulders to safety. In the effort of bringing in the wounded in the face of the enemy, Fraser felt that the Germans treated them fairly. In May 1917 he was killed in the Second Battle of Bullecourt (stage 11) and his name is engraved on the Memorial Wall at Villers-Bretonneux (stage 9) because his remains were never found.

5 German army records, historical research and aerial photography confirmed the presence of bodies in mass graves that were never recovered, just outside the village. In May 2008 it was decided to exhume, identify and bury the bodies individually in a new cemetery. Thanks to historical, anthropological, archaeological and DNA evidence, 125 of the headstones now have a name, but just as many simply read "Known unto God", the standard phrase used for unknown soldiers.

Mountain bikes will have no difficulties here but those on racing bikes will want to ride around this section.

◆ The route takes you along *Rue de la Biette* and passes the recycling park. *Rue Deleval* leads to the church and bypasses the narrow stone path that cuts through the field.

6 Ride parallel to the crest and join Rue Basse, which leads to the D41, where you turn left and immediately right again after 200m to continue in the same direction down Rue du Bas Pommereau. Go left at the wood along Chemin de Ligny. At the end of that street turn left onto the D72 for 100m before turning right into Rue du Moulin to reach the D167. Cross the D947 and continue until you reach the canal. Here nothing remains to remind you of this forgotten sector of the front where the soldiers hated the rats more than they hated the Germans.

Hill 70

In the spring of 1915 the British sector went from the north of Ypres all the way to Lens in the south. The Germans occupied the city and the higher ground before Lens, from where they had a clear field of observation over the surrounding Douai Plains with their strategic coal reserves.

In September 1915 the Battle of Loos was the British component of the combined Anglo-French offensive that aimed to support the French during their second large-scale attack on Vimy Ridge. It involved six divisions and was the largest British offensive mounted on the Western Front in 1915. The German defensive lines were situated on Hill 70.

The Double Crassier.

Lens
9
8
M
Marquillies
Salomé
Wingles
Herlies
Douvrin
Hulluch
Ligny-
le-Grand
Illies
La
Bassée
Le
Bourg
Ligny-
le-Petit
Haisnes
Loos-
en-Gohelle
PAS-DE-
CALAIS
Violaines
Auchy-
les-Mines
La
Rutoire
Lorgies
Liévin
7
Grenay
Vermelles
Neuve-
Chapelle
Givenchy-
la-Bassée
Canal d'Aire à la Bassée
Festubert
6
Guinchy
Noyelles-
lès-Vermelles
Mazingarbe
Cambrin
9,6 km
5,3 km
4,8 km
6,8 km
5,8 km
N 41
N 47
A 211
A 21
D 141
D 947
D 165
D 163
D 39
D 58
D 168
D 72
D 75
D 167
D 167E
D 941
D 943
D 166
D 171
D 170
D 165E1
N
S
E
O
0
1
2 km
Nieupoort
BELGIQUE
Calais
Dunkerque
Ypres
Courtrai
PAS-DE-
CALAIS
Armentières
Lille
Boulogne-
sur-Mer
Lens
Arras
Scarpe
NORD
Cambrai
Abbeville
SOMME
Somme
Amiens
St-Quentin
Lys
Escaut

The Battle of Loos

Early in the morning on 25 September 1915, 140 tons of gas were released by British forces. When the battle opened the first German line was taken but the losses were very high. The advance came to a halt, however, when the wind turned and blew the gas back into the British lines, killing more than 2,600. The Germans reclaimed Hill 70 and, with fresh reserves, pushed back the British attacks. Some of the ground gained on the first day was lost again. The fighting subsided with the British having retreated on their starting positions. Later subsidiary attacks failed.

7 From Vermelles the path at the end of Rue Duquesne is no longer asphalted so you make a right turn onto the busy D943. The cycle lane makes it safe enough to ride to "Dud Corner".

8 Behind the memorial a country road takes you to Loos and onto *Rue Salengro*, with its long

Dud Corner Cemetery and Loos Memorial

The total British casualties were 59,247. Because of the large number of unexploded shells that were found while building this cemetery it was named "Dud Corner". The screen wall is the Loos Memorial that commemorates the 20,605 who do not have a known grave and fell here in the battles. Of all the regiments listed, five Scottish regiments are most represented. John Kipling, the only son of the author and poet Rudyard Kipling, was serving with the 2nd Battalion Irish Guards when he was killed and the whereabouts of his body are not known. His name can be found on panel 9.

Coal mining

The first pit opened in 1851 and with new technology the extraction of coal soon turned this formerly quiet farming area into one of the most industrialised parts of France. In 1906 a coal dust explosion was heard and the Courrières mine disaster, Europe's worst mining accident, caused the death of 1,099 miners. Many of the miners were children and the public emotion combined with the slow progress of the rescue caused unrest and political crisis. Mining continued here until 1972 when the last mine pit closed.

Jean Jaurès

An eloquent speaker, journalist, founder of the French newspaper *L'Humanité* and a prominent socialist leader, Jean Jaurès was sensitive to the conditions of the working class. After the mine disaster and during the strike against the government, he took the side of the mine workers against Interior Minister Georges Clemenceau. Jaurès was a committed antimilitarist who tried to use diplomatic means to prevent what became the First World War. He was assassinated in a Parisian café by Raoul Villain, a French nationalist. Villain was tried after World War I and acquitted.

The recent inauguration of this new museum has provided a boost to the economy of an area that has never fully recovered from the mine closures. Do take your time to admire the interesting architecture of the museum, but please note that you should not ride your bike within the museum grounds.

rows of brick houses in the former miners' neighbourhoods, until you finally reach the D943, which you follow downhill for a few hundred yards. At the hotel you turn right into the large parking area of the "Bollaert" football stadium and the recently inaugurated Louvre-Lens museum.

◆ Lens was devastated more than any other city in France during World War I. It was completely flattened, with not one house left standing. As in Ypres, reconstruction work started in the years after the war, but the Second World War again took a heavy toll here for it was an important railway centre. Saint-Léger church has been rebuilt to look identical to the pre-war church.

9 The railway station is an illustration of the reborn city of Lens. The architect did not want it to look like any other station. The Art Deco concrete construction suggests a steam locomotive with its tower as the chimney. At its inauguration the design was highly controversial but today it has become an icon of the city and a central point for getting to and from the new museum.

In the railway station, unique Art Deco mosaics represent the glory days of the mining industry.

Stage 6

From Lens to Arras

The hills of Artois

45km

This stage involves riding on a heap of spoil and waste rock, climbing three decent hills, enjoying impressive panoramas and exploring two major historic sites of the First World War. It is relatively short but rather challenging and also one of the richest stages in terms of historical interest.

Every year, thousands of French and foreign travellers visit this area, but to Canadians a visit to this ridge is a pilgrimage. In an admirably well-kept park a modern welcome centre reveals the significance that this place holds. Your physical efforts to climb the ridge will be well worth it!

The Chemin du Mont Guyot… up to the top of the hill!

❶ Rather than riding through the busy railway tunnel to leave Lens centre it is better to walk along the footpath on the opposite side of the road so that you will be at the right side of the D58E to join *Rue Arthur Fauqueur* on your left.

❷ Take the cycle bridge across the *Route d'Arras* and from there a 5km cycle route will take you over a slag heap to the town of Angres, at the foot of the ridge. At the first traffic lights, turn right onto the D51 and continue for 3.2km. At the end of the road, turn right and stay on the D937 for 1.2km. The heavy, busy traffic requires your full attention here!

❸ *Rue Zeffe* and *Rue Lantoine* make it possible to ride parallel to the D937 and join the D165 to Bouvigny. In that village, look for *Rue Salvador Allende* and prepare for a short but stiff climb up the ridge. *Chemin des Loups* on the crest offers a spectacular panorama of the surrounding mining area and in clear weather the hills south of Ypres can be spotted in the far distance.

A strategic vantage point

Taken and occupied by the enemy in October 1914, this ridge was one of the most crucial positions in the German defence system. Not only did it offer a perfect vantage point over the town of Arras but it also gave commanding views over the minefields and energy reserves that lay between Lens and Douai. Two Franco-British attacks to recapture it proved unsuccessful and cost over 150,000 casualties.

Hill 119 or "The Pimple".

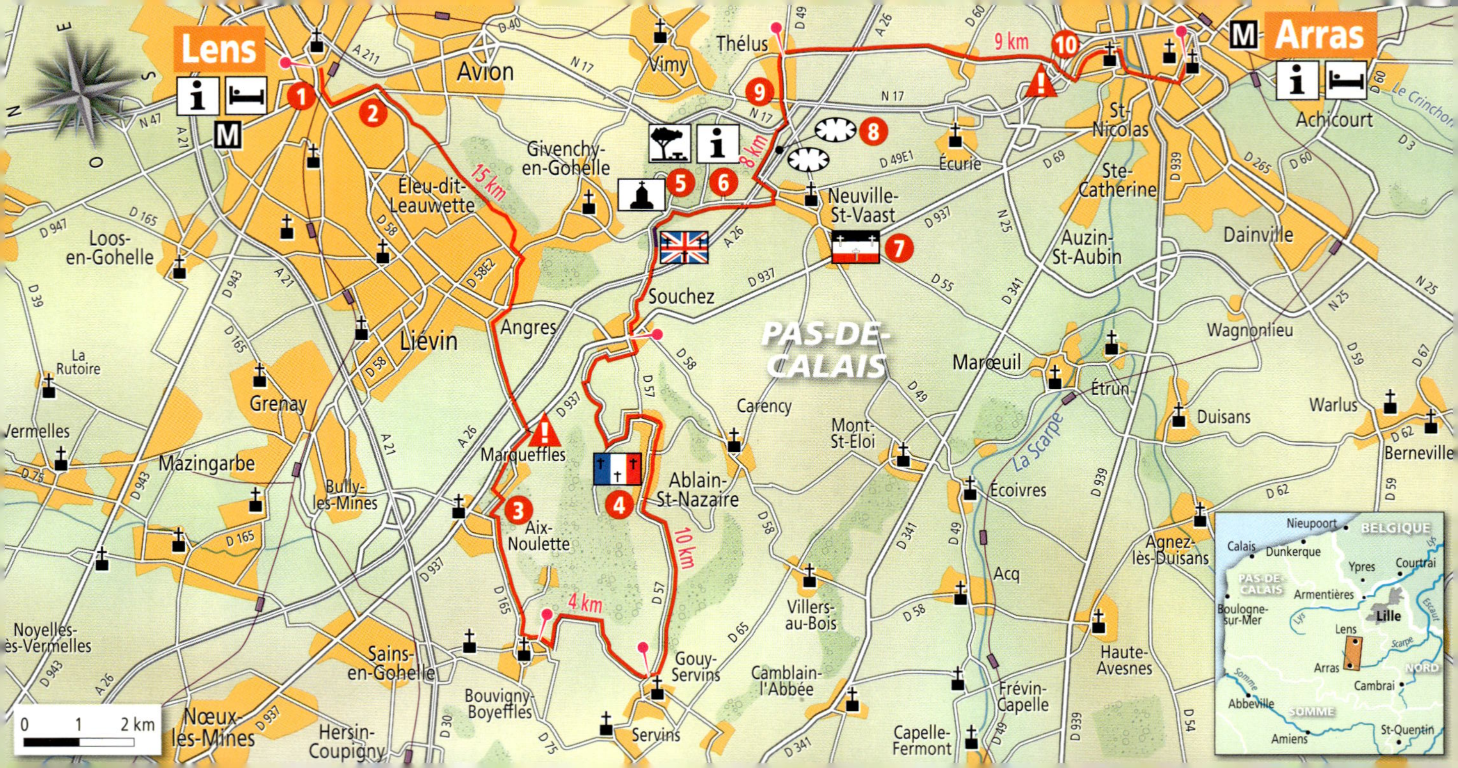

Lens
Arras
Avion
Vimy
Thélus
Givenchy-en-Gohelle
Éleu-dit-Leauwette
Loos-en-Gohelle
Liévin
Angres
Souchez
Neuville-St-Vaast
Écurie
St-Nicolas
Ste-Catherine
Achicourt
Dainville
Auzin-St-Aubin
Wagnonlieu
Marœuil
Étrun
Duisans
Warlus
Berneville
PAS-DE-CALAIS
Carency
Mont-St-Éloi
Écoivres
Agnez-lès-Duisans
Acq
Villers-au-Bois
Haute-Avesnes
Frévin-Capelle
Camblain-l'Abbée
Capelle-Fermont
Gouy-Servins
Servins
Ablain-St-Nazaire
Aix-Noulette
Marqueffles
Bouvigny-Boyeffles
Sains-en-Gohelle
Hersin-Coupigny
Nœux-les-Mines
Bully-les-Mines
Grenay
Mazingarbe
La Rutoire
Vermelles
Noyelles-lès-Vermelles
La Scarpe
Le Crinchon
15 km
8 km
9 km
10 km
4 km
0 1 2 km
A 211
A 21
A 26
N 17
N 47
N 25
D 40
D 49
D 60
D 3
D 265
D 939
D 69
D 49E1
D 937
D 55
D 341
D 58
D 58E2
D 57
D 165
D 947
D 943
D 39
D 75
D 30
D 65
D 59
D 67
D 62
D 54
Nieuport
BELGIQUE
Calais
Dunkerque
Ypres
Courtrai
PAS-DE-CALAIS
Armentières
Lille
Boulogne-sur-Mer
Lens
Arras
Cambrai
NORD
Abbeville
SOMME
Amiens
St-Quentin
Lys
Escaut
Scarpe
Somme

The First Battle of Arras

The French Commander-in-Chief, Joffre, wanted to release pressure on the Russians and exploit the diversion of German troops to the Eastern Front by punching a hole in the German defences here, on the Western Front. In the spring of 1915 the French and British launched a joint attack over a 20km-wide front between Arras and Aubers. The French army attacked north of Arras and took the 16km-long (10 mile) ridge. The British army attacked on the same day on the left flank and widened the gap. The French artillery preparations were in the key sector of the 33rd French Army Corps under Pétain, who secured a remarkable success.

(4) Only mountain bikes can ride the crest all the way; other cyclists should turn right and ride downhill and then turn left onto the D57 towards Ablain-Saint-Nazaire. After 5km, where you see a church in ruins, turn left for a second climb up the steep slopes to the chapel of Notre-Dame de Lorette.

◆ The small military cemetery that was set up by French soldiers after the battle was later chosen to become a major burial site known as Notre-Dame de Lorette. It holds the remains of 40,000 French soldiers. A new chapel and a lighthouse were also erected to commemorate the fallen.

Ablain-Saint-Nazaire and its church in ruins.

Notre-Dame de Lorette

The 77th Division commandeered by General Barbot took Souchez and in the same dash pushed its way up to Hill 119, where the division was checked by the enemy and had to fall back. General Barbot was fatally wounded. As part of that same push the Moroccan Division reached the crest of Vimy Ridge, but it was too far from its bases (12km) without supplies and could not hold its ground when the Germans counter-attacked; it was forced to backpedal to the foot of the hill. It took another month of bitter fighting to capture and secure the hill of Notre-Dame de Lorette but the crucial position of Vimy remained in German hands.

Notre-Dame de Lorette.

The Second Battle of Arras

(also known as the Loos-Artois Offensive)

Following a four-day artillery bombardment starting on 21 September 1915, a second large-scale Franco-British offensive aimed to take the ridge. The French took their first objectives and the initial success of the British divisions at Loos offered hope for future successes. By 26 September the French had taken the village of Souchez but had made little progress south-east of Neuville-Saint-Vaast. The French failed to breach the German second line of defence and a breakthrough could not be achieved. The pressure on the Russians was released but none of the objectives were achieved.

The stained-glass windows in the basilica show the French fighting bravely from their trenches. In a wooden cabinet behind a glass door hangs the wooden cross that stood on the grave of Louise de Bettignies in Cologne (see stage 1).

◆ Among the countless plaques we find the name of François Faber, who won five stages in the Tour de France and took the yellow jersey in 1909. He was the first non-Frenchman to win that prize. As a former dockworker, born of a French mother and a Luxembourg father, the "giant of Colombes" was a Luxembourg national. He enlisted in the French Foreign Legion and fell here in May 1915.

Plaques with the names of fallen soldiers were put up on the wall of the basilica by their families.

◆ The local museum on the ridge, next to the restaurant, has a collection of more than 2,000 pieces but the most interesting part is the preserved battleground with the original trenches, French and German guns and howitzers, machine guns, shells, barbed wire and armoured turrets. The explanatory boards are in French, English and German.

The **musée vivant 1914-1918.**

5 Take the cycle lane downhill on the main road. Before you arrive at the busy D937, turn right into Rue du Docteur Henri Wagon and head along Rue du Maréchal Leclerc to make your way to the lovely town hall of Souchez. Cross the D937 to the church on Rue du 19 Mars 1962 and follow the CWGC signs (Givenchy Road Canadian Cemetery) for your third climb of the day up the steep slopes of Vimy Ridge. At the end of the dirt trail, turn right to find the Canadian Monument.

The Third Battle of Arras

The 1917 British offensive was on a relatively broad front between Vimy in the north-west and Bullecourt (see stage 11) in the south-east. At the same time the operation released pressure on the French who were fighting at the Chemin des Dames under General Nivelles.

Under the cover of a perfectly orchestrated bombardment, Canadian troops advancing in the north were able to capture the strategically significant Vimy Ridge and British divisions in the centre were also able to make significant gains astride the river Scarpe. In the south, British and Australian forces were frustrated by the elastic defence and made only minimal gains.

The preliminary phase

Before the action could be undertaken, a great deal of preparation was required, much of it highly innovative. For years, French and later British engineers had been working underground to construct tunnels and subways for the troops to move forwards and the wounded to be evacuated. The plan was well developed, drawing on the lessons of the Somme the previous year. To keep enemy action to a minimum during the assault an artillery barrage was planned to come down like a curtain on the German positions and to creep across the battlefield 100 yards every 3 minutes in advance of the assaulting troops.

Canadian success on Vimy Ridge

Three Canadian divisions captured their objectives on the first day; only the 4th Division encountered a great deal of trouble by insistent German fire from the "Pimple". On the second day the crest of Hill 145 was captured. That is where the monument stands today. In four days the Canadians had successfully captured all their objectives. In the centre, astride the river Scarpe, a 5km advance was made in two days, but then the fighting subsided. Southern British and Australian divisions stormed the Hindenburg line, suffering terrible losses but making very little or no headway (see Bullecourt, stage 11).

The pylons, one bearing the maple leaf for Canada and the other the fleur-de-lis for France, symbolise the unity and sacrifice of both countries.

The Canadian Monument and Memorial Park

In 1922 the French Government granted an area of land on the crest of the ridge to the Canadian nation "in perpetuity". The monument itself was constructed on Hill 145, so called because it was the highest point of Vimy Ridge at 145 metres above sea level. On the walls are engraved the names of 11,285 Canadians who do not have a known grave. King Edward VIII unveiled the memorial in 1936. In 1996 the Vimy Memorial and the battlefield site surrounding it was established as a National Historic Site of Canada. After a massive restoration project over several years the memorial was rededicated on the 90th anniversary of the battle, on 9 April 2007.

The grieving figure of Mother Canada, oriented to face the dawn of a new day, is an allegorical representation of the young Canadian nation mourning its lost sons.

On the west side of the memorial, one male and one female figure recline on either side of the steps. They represent the mourning mothers and fathers of fallen soldiers. The artist's underlying message reminds us of the grieving parents sculpture by Käthe Kollwitz (stage 2).

❻ The Canadian Welcome Centre is open every day from 9:00am to 5:00pm and at the desk you can book a guided visit to a section of the underground tunnels, no man's land, the observation posts and the trenches where the assault troops went over the top. The best way to organise your visit is to start by going to the desk and arranging with the guide when you can book this 1-hour tour. If you have to wait a while, you can visit the memorial before the tour or take some time to have a rest, use the wooden tables for your picnic and make use of the excellent facilities that are free of charge.

❼ From the Welcome Centre, turn left onto the D55 and pass the A26 motorway. Unless you want the visit the largest German military cemetery in France, turn left after the bridge to Litchfield Crater. To visit the German cemetery, stay on the D55 until you reach Neuville-Saint-Vaast town hall, church, square and school, where you head along Rue du 8 Mai. This farm road takes you across the old battlefield. The plot with trees is the final resting place for 44,833 German soldiers. The contrast with the Commonwealth cemeteries couldn't be more striking.

The German military cemetery at Neuville-Saint-Vaast.

The words Ich hatt' einen Kameraden or "I had a comrade", engraved on the monument in the centre, refer to an old poem and lament, which plays an important ceremonial role – it is an integral part of German military funerals and is also sung on German Remembrance Day.

❽ The country road passes in front of Litchfield Crater, one of two mine craters (the other being Zivy Crater) which were used by the Canadian Corps Burial Officer in 1917 for the burial of bodies found on the Vimy battlefield. The crater is essentially a mass grave and contains 57 First World War burials, 15 of them unidentified.

Lichfield Crater.

The Canadian Artillery Memorial.

9 The Canadian Artillery Memorial is located at the traffic lights and busy crossroads. It is hardly as elegant at the Vimy Memorial and testifies to the key role of the engineers in the preparation and execution of the creeping barrage.

10 From the ridge north of Arras the route goes via Thélus downhill to Roclincourt. Take the bridge over the N17 and at the roundabout stay parallel to the N17 all the way down to the river Scarpe, where you ride along the towpath to Arras.

Town Hall.

Arras

At the confluence of the Crinchon and the Scarpe, the town of Arras, just like Ypres, was a thriving textile centre during the Middle Ages. Its textiles were known in Italy as *Arazzi*. By the end of the 15th century, grain had replaced textiles. The old cloth hall gave way to the new belfry tower in the Flamboyant Gothic style.

Remaining in Allied hands during the war, it was less than 10km from the front line that formed a salient into enemy lines. For more than 30 long months Arras was within range of the German artillery and three-quarters of the city was destroyed.

Arras tourist office is in the historic town hall in front of the belfry tower (www.arras.fr).

Stage 7

From Arras to Albert

From the Scarpe valley to the Ancre valley

45km

This stage links Arras to Albert and also connects the Scarpe valley to the Ancre valley, two very different areas. You will trade the highly industrialised Artois for the rolling fields and fertile farmland of Picardy.

A new page and a new chapter open up. In the fields of the Somme, impressive monuments and excellent visitor centres tell the story of the Allies' hopes of ending this war here in 1916 with a Franco-British offensive that aimed to free France of German occupation. At the same time the Germans launched an offensive on Verdun, also with the hope of ending the war.

The track along the Crinchon.

Arras, the garrison town

The Germans had entered Arras and some 3,000 men occupied the barracks of the citadel to install their headquarters there. French units under General Maud'huy pushed the enemy back and dug trenches at the outskirts to defend the town. Arras remained in Allied hands and in 1916 the Commonwealth Army took over this sector from the French. Arras became the logistical centre for a broad front assault between Vimy in the north-west and Bullecourt in the south-east. After the war the town was rebuilt to look the same as it had before the conflict.

Faubourg d'Amiens Cemetery and Arras Memorial.

❶ Your route starts at the citadel with the adjacent Faubourg d'Amiens Cemetery and Arras Memorial and the *Mur des Fusillés* at the back of the citadel.

◆ During the first two years of the war the French buried their dead at the east side of the city, along the ring road. When the British imperial forces took over this sector a new cemetery, adjacent to the French burial ground, was opened and later enlarged with the graves of victims of the Battle of Arras. When the French exhumed their soldiers to concentrate the graves at Notre-Dame de Lorette, Britain decided to build a memorial to its 35,000 missing in this sector. The number is almost identical to Tyne Cot Cemetery near Passendale (stage 3).

◆ Upon entering the cemetery a bay is dedicated to the commemoration of 991 airmen with no known grave. The Arras Flying Services Memorial is in the form of an obelisk with a globe which forms a finial on the top. The names of Commonwealth pilots are engraved on the four sides. Lanoe George Hawker VC, DSO was a British flying ace during the First World War.

The Arras Flying Services Memorial.

He was the first British flying ace and the third pilot to receive the Victoria Cross. He was killed in a dog fight with the legendary German ace Manfred von Richthofen, also known as the Red Baron (or the "Red Devil" by the French).

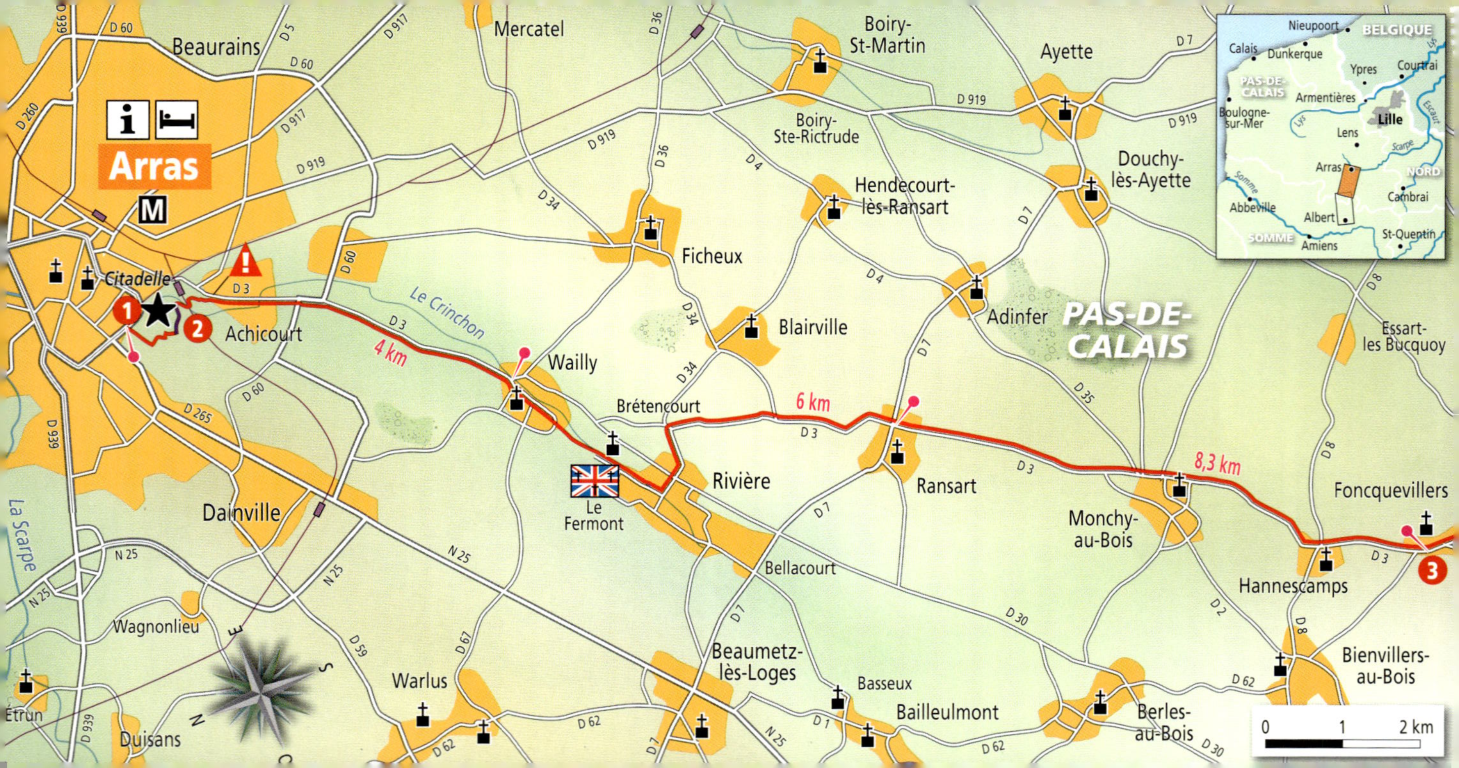

Arras
Beaurains
Mercatel
Boiry-St-Martin
Ayette
Boiry-Ste-Rictrude
Douchy-lès-Ayette
Hendecourt-lès-Ransart
Ficheux
Citadelle
Achicourt
Le Crinchon
4 km
Wailly
Blairville
Adinfer
PAS-DE-CALAIS
Essart-les Bucquoy
Brétencourt
6 km
Le Fermont
Rivière
Ransart
8,3 km
Foncquevillers
Monchy-au-Bois
Hannescamps
Dainville
Bellacourt
Wagnonlieu
Warlus
Beaumetz-lès-Loges
Basseux
Bailleulmont
Berles-au-Bois
Bienvillers-au-Bois
Étrun
Duisans
La Scarpe
D 60
D 5
D 917
D 36
D 7
D 919
D 260
D 3
D 34
D 4
D 8
D 35
D 939
D 265
N 25
D 59
D 67
D 62
D 1
D 30
D 2
0
1
2 km
Nieuport
BELGIQUE
Calais
Dunkerque
Ypres
Courtrai
PAS-DE-CALAIS
Armentières
Lille
Boulogne-sur-Mer
Lens
Scarpe
Escaut
Lys
Arras
NORD
Somme
Abbeville
Cambrai
Albert
SOMME
Amiens
St-Quentin

The mur des Fusillés.

◆ During the Second World War the Germans used the citadel as barracks. In the dry moat behind the citadel they executed 218 French Resistance fighters. After being a French army base for many decades, the citadel became part of the city in 2010 and is now open to the public. To access the execution area you ride into the citadel and leave it by the gate on the south side.

❷ Enter the park behind the citadel and follow the path alongside the star-shaped moat until you reach the river Crinchon, where you turn right onto the railway crossing. Turn left immediately and look for a path on your right, around 80 yards further on. This path takes you through the allotments of Achicourt to the roundabout, where you turn onto the D3 for around 4km to Wailly.

◆ At the church of Wailly you don't stay on the D3 but go straight on and follow the Crinchon again for 2.5km before turning left at the little bridge over the river. At the junction with the D30 in Brétencourt you rejoin the D3 and go south for 11km.

❸ In Foncquevillers, behind the church, a granite plaque commemorates the crew of a Halifax bomber plane that crashed nearby in June 1944. From Foncquevillers, take the D6 to Gommecourt.

◆ Before leaving the village of Gommecourt, turn left into the *Chemin d'Hébuterne*. A little further on you will see the white headstones of a military cemetery in the green fields in the middle of the no man's land between the two villages of Gommecourt and Hébuterne.

The Somme

After the 1914 German defeat on the Marne, the Somme front was formed and stabilised by the winter. The enemy established solid defences on every hilltop that became fortified strongholds. Gommecourt was in German hands and the lines bulged, forming salients into the Allied lines at Hébuterne. About eight miles north of Albert, an additional operation took place. Two divisions of territorials aimed to draw some German reserves away from the main Somme offensive further south and also to try to eliminate the German salient in the lines here. They did not receive any artillery support and were decimated on the first day of the battle.

The Franco-British offensive in the Somme

In 1916 the French (Joffre) convinced the British (Haig) to approve the plan for a joint military operation in the Somme. The convergence of French and British efforts would guarantee the success of this operation and the chiefs of staff started drawing up plans. Bapaume was the objective set for the British forces and Péronne became the French objective. Three days after the agreement was sealed a sudden and unexpected event occurred when the Germans opened a new front on the Meuse in Verdun. The French reduced their troops in the Somme sector to compensate for the losses, and the urgency of the offensive increased.

The Halifax and crew.

◆ In Hébuterne, rather than following the D28 or the D27, take the *Rue de Serre* and ride to Touvent Farm. A track cuts through the fields and takes you to Sheffield Park and the adjacent cemetery. A city bike can ride this track but those on racing bikes will have to ride to the D919.

❹ In Sheffield Park you will find an old shallow trench that formed the jumping-off point for the Pals battalions. A stainless steel plaque gives detailed information about the trenches and what happened here on 1 July 1916.

◆ With some 63 identified casualties, Railway Hollow Cemetery is situated in an enclosure behind the park. In the first row the epitaph on the grave of Alfred Goodlad is moving and worth reading. It was the first time he had left his country, and in his

The Accrington Pals

letter to his mother he wrote of how impressed he was: "The French are a great nation worth fighting for". He was one of the 60,000 casualties on the first day of the battle and his parents later had his words engraved on his headstone.

◆ Rather than assigning the new recruits to work alongside

experienced men from the existing army, Kitchener promised men who enlisted together in local recruiting drives that they would be able to serve alongside their friends, neighbours, work colleagues and family members. Before the winter of 1914, over fifty towns had formed "Pals battalions", with larger towns and cities each able to form several battalions.

"Featherbed soldiers"

Contrary to the popular view that the war would soon be over, Kitchener predicted a long war and believed that only a massive force of new divisions could defeat the Central Powers on the continent. The enthusiastic civilian recruits that formed the New Army were seen by the professionals in the British Expeditionary Force as "featherbed soldiers"!

❺ The trail brings you back to the D919. Just 500m further on, a French cemetery reminds us that this was indeed a French sector in 1915. The road to Beaumont goes left, before arriving at the British cemetery.

Plaque with a French grenadier at the Serre French military cemetery.

The cemetery marks the middle of the no man's land between the lines.

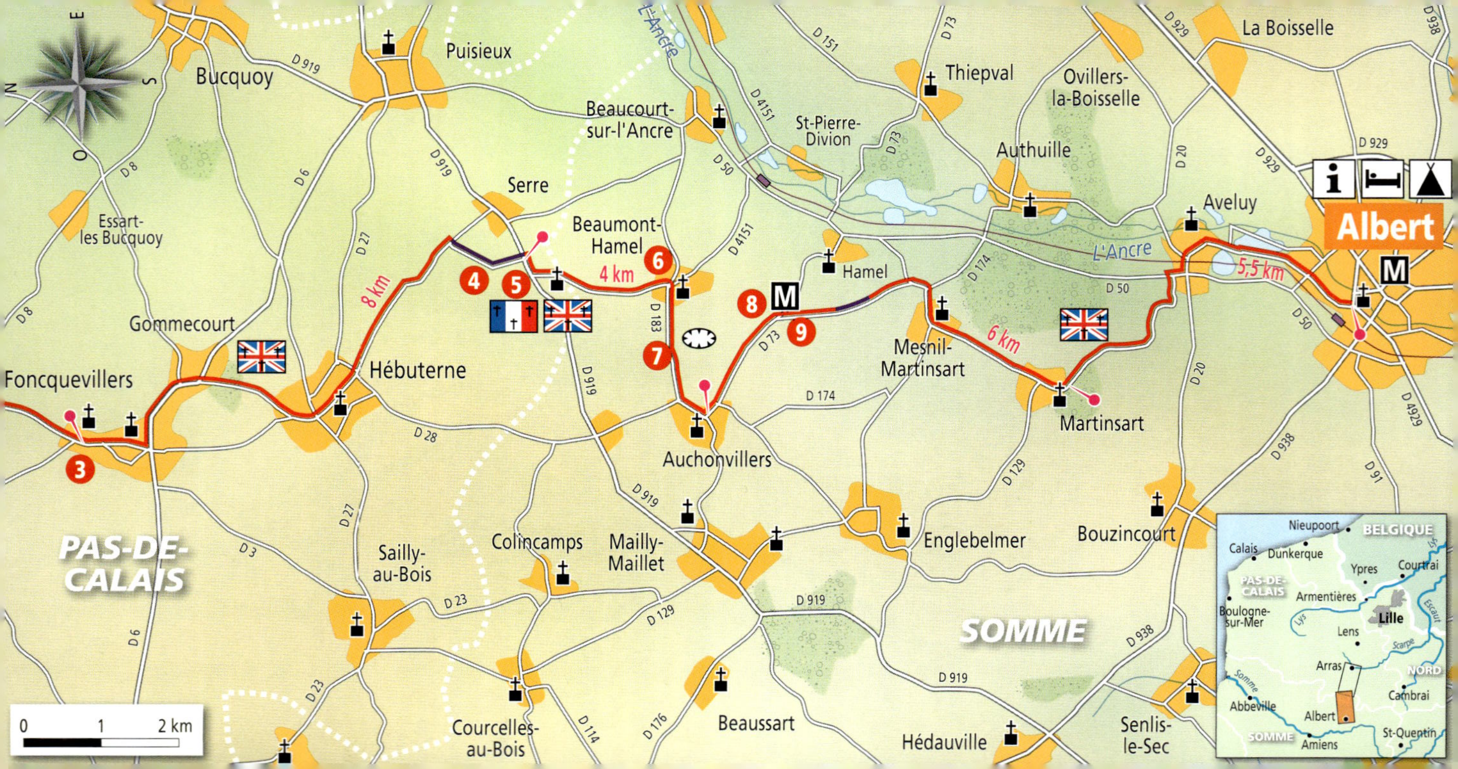

Albert
La Boisselle
Ovillers-la-Boisselle
Thiepval
Puisieux
Bucquoy
Beaucourt-sur-l'Ancre
St-Pierre-Divion
Authuille
Aveluy
Serre
Beaumont-Hamel
Hamel
Essart-les Bucquoy
Gommecourt
Foncquevillers
Hébuterne
Mesnil-Martinsart
Martinsart
Auchonvillers
Colincamps
Mailly-Maillet
Sailly-au-Bois
Englebelmer
Bouzincourt
Courcelles-au-Bois
Beaussart
Hédauville
Senlis-le-Sec
PAS-DE-CALAIS
SOMME
L'Ancre
8 km
4 km
6 km
5,5 km
D 919
D 929
D 938
D 4929
D 91
D 50
D 20
D 151
D 73
D 4151
D 174
D 183
D 129
D 8
D 6
D 27
D 28
D 3
D 23
D 114
D 176
0
1
2 km
Nieupoort
BELGIQUE
Calais
Dunkerque
Ypres
Courtrai
PAS-DE-CALAIS
Armentières
Boulogne-sur-Mer
Lille
Lens
Escaut
Scarpe
Lys
Arras
NORD
Cambrai
Somme
Abbeville
Albert
SOMME
Amiens
St-Quentin

The 51st Celtic Cross Memorial.

6 From Beaumont to Auchonvillers you ride from the old German line straight to the former British lines. Where the Celtic cross overlooks the no man's land, the sunken road was the jumping-off point on the morning of the first day of the battle.

◆ In Auchonvillers, Avril Williams' tearoom deserves to be mentioned for her friendly greeting and informative local knowledge.

7 After more than four months of fighting, the 51st Highlander Division finally managed to capture the first German line and the village of Beaumont was liberated on 13 November. Seven days later the Battle of the Somme officially ended.

8 From the sunken road, take the road to Auchonvillers, then turn left and follow the signs for Newfoundland Memorial Park. The initiative to purchase this land came from mothers, widows and a priest who wanted to preserve the field where their men died. Today it is the largest preserved area of the Somme battleground.

60,000 casualties on 1 July 1916

The officers tried to compensate the inexperience of the new troops by planning the battle methodically and in the finest detail. The expectation was that the ferocity of the preliminary artillery bombardment would entirely destroy all forward German defences and enable the infantry to practically walk across no man's land and take the German trenches. When the first attacking wave of infantrymen went over the top, the attack was by no means a surprise to the German forces. On the first day of the Battle of the Somme, many troops were killed or wounded the moment they stepped out of the front lines into no man's land. They made incredibly easy targets for the German machine gunners.

The Newfoundland Regiment

When the Newfoundland Regiment received orders to move forward on the first day of the battle, the communication trenches were congested with dead and wounded so they had to move immediately into attack formation and advance across the surface, which first involved navigating through the British barbed wire defences. As they breasted the skyline behind the British first line, they were clearly visible to the German defenders. Most of the Newfoundland Regiment were dead, dying or wounded within 15 to 20 minutes. The Newfoundland Regiment had been wiped out, the unit as a whole having suffered a casualty rate of approximately 80%.

The Caribou.

◆ Visiting the field and the visitor centre with its maps and excellent explanations will help you gain a better understanding of the tragedy that unfolded here a century ago.

◆ The memorial is one of six erected by the Government of Newfoundland after the First World War. The bronze caribou, the emblem of the Royal Newfoundland Regiment, stands atop an artificial hill that offers visitors a comprehensive view over the old battlefield.

The Highlander.

◆ At the base of the Beaumont-Hamel Newfoundland Memorial mound the bronze tables list the names of those with no known grave. The statue of the Highlander is situated at the back of the park overlooking Y Ravine, the scene of fierce fighting on

The Golden Virgin.

13 November when Beaumont was captured.

⑨ Just 300m after leaving the park, a country road on your right takes you to Mesnil. As you ride downhill to the valley of the Ancre, the panorama of the opposite riverbank and the monument above the tree line is stunning. The strategic position of this high ground becomes obvious when you realise that it was such an ideal observation point. In Mesnil, do not turn left onto the D174 but continue straight down to Martinsart and then the D50. After 250m turn left onto the D20 and almost immediately right to ride parallel to the railway line, along the lakes, towards the centre of Albert.

◆ The spire of the basilica of Notre-Dame de Brebières and the gold-plated statue of Mary and the infant Jesus forming a finial was a striking sight in the Somme, serving as a beacon that could be observed from most positions in the northern half of the Somme front.

◆ In 1915 the top of the basilica was hit by a German shell and the statue slumped to a near-horizontal position. A number of legends surrounding the "Leaning Virgin" developed among the soldiers, and it was said that whoever knocked down the statue would lose the war.

◆ At the foot of the basilica is the entrance to the Somme Trench Museum (the *Musée Somme 1916*). It is housed underground in a former WWII bomb shelter, the perfect place to recreate the life of men in the dugouts and shelters (www.musee-somme-1916.eu).

The Somme Trench Museum.

Stage 8

Thiepval Ridge and Pozières

The 1916 Somme Remembrance Trail

33km, centre based

This centre-based tour over the beautiful rolling hills of the Somme will lead you to key remembrance sites where you can learn about the different phases of the Battle of the Somme. This may be the shortest of all the stages but it is certainly the richest in history. Two outings also link this stage to Bapaume and back to Arras, or to Péronne, making it possible to create a much longer tour.

The main subject is the 1916 Battle of the Somme, and you will visit all the 'must sees' on the remembrance trail.

At the end of a long and steady rise, Thiepval Ridge and its visitor centre.

❶ You could start on the D942 and take the *Chemin d'Authuille*, but it is much more fun to make your way through the town via *Avenue Lomont* and *Avenue Dunant*. The little country road passes the site where legend has it that the statue of Notre-Dame de Brebières was found by a shepherd. In your long climb up to the Thiepval crest, try not to forget to enjoy the wonderful panoramas and admire the Douglas Fir in Newfoundland Park on the horizon.

❷ About 300 yards before the red brick church of Thiepval, on your right you will come to Thiepval Visitor Centre. The explanatory panels in three languages

– English, French and German – provide an overview of the course of the Great War from 1914 to 1918. There are various facilities, including an information desk, shop, and food and drink dispensers, and the patio on top of the washrooms makes a perfect picnic area.

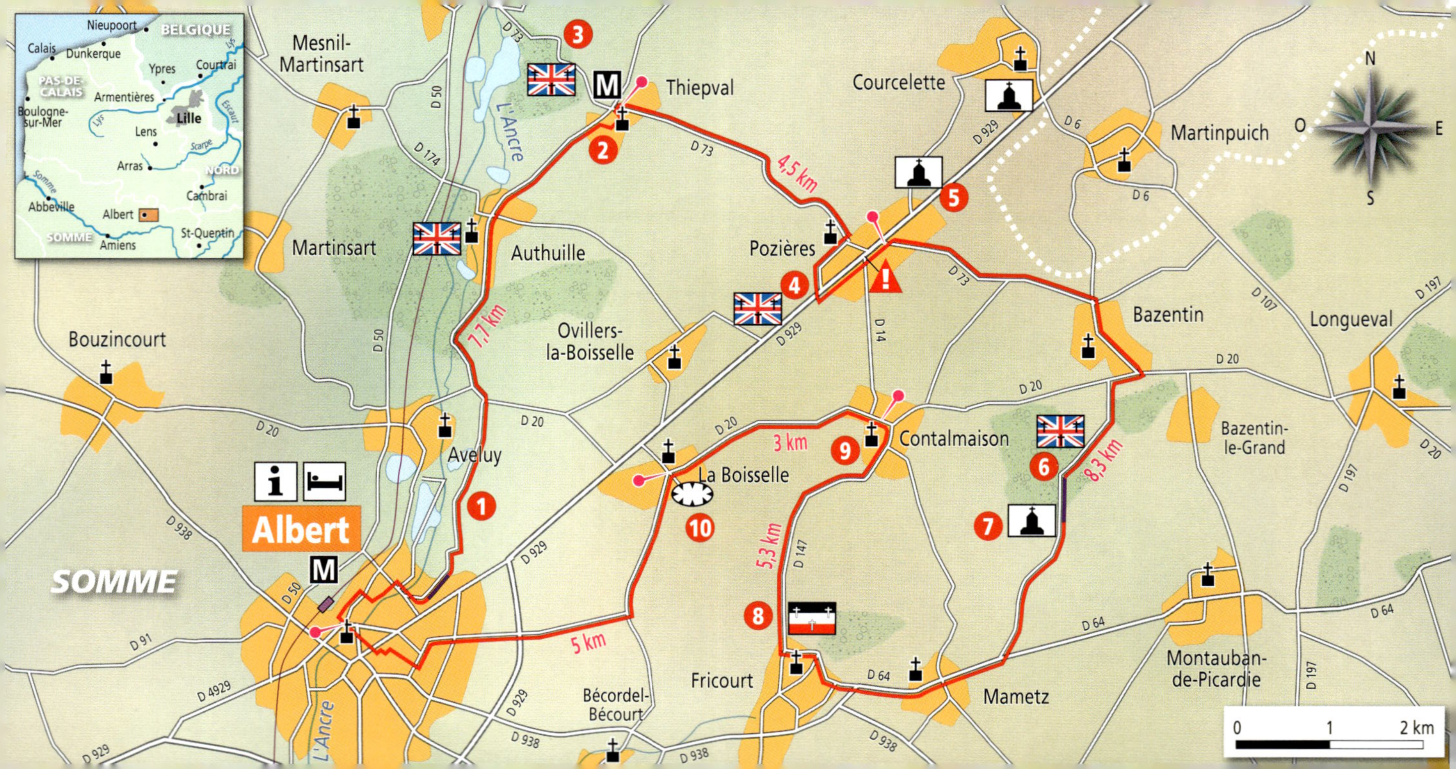
Nieupoort
BELGIQUE
Calais
Dunkerque
Ypres
Courtrai
PAS-DE-CALAIS
Armentières
Boulogne-sur-Mer
Lille
Lys
Escaut
Lens
Scarpe
Arras
NORD
Somme
Cambrai
Abbeville
Albert
SOMME
Amiens
St-Quentin
Mesnil-Martinsart
Thiepval
Courcelette
Martinpuich
Martinsart
Authuille
Pozières
Bazentin
Longueval
Bouzincourt
Ovillers-la-Boisselle
Contalmaison
Bazentin-le-Grand
Aveluy
La Boisselle
Albert
SOMME
Fricourt
Mametz
Montauban-de-Picardie
Bécordel-Bécourt
L'Ancre
D 73
D 50
D 174
D 929
D 6
D 107
D 197
D 14
D 20
D 147
D 64
D 938
D 91
D 4929
4,5 km
7,7 km
3 km
8,3 km
5,3 km
5 km
1
2
3
4
5
6
7
8
9
10
M
N
O
E
S
0
1
2 km

The Battle of Thiepval Ridge

Thiepval Ridge was a well-fortified strategic element in the German defences overlooking the Ancre valley in the north and Pozières in the south. It was the objective of the first day of the battle but the German defenders fought with great determination, while the coordination of British infantry and artillery deteriorated after the first day due to the confused nature of the fighting in the mazes of trenches, dugouts and shell craters. After Pozières was retaken, British operations on 30 September concluded with the capture of a large portion of the Schwaben Redoubt. The rest of Schwaben Redoubt was captured on 14 October.

Commemoration Site

Because of the significance of Thiepval Ridge, the high ground on the spur was chosen to house the Memorial to the Missing of the Somme. With 73,367 names engraved on the white panels it is the largest Commonwealth memorial in the world. To symbolise the alliance between France and Great Britain in this battle it was agreed that 300 French soldiers should be buried side by side with 300 Commonwealth soldiers, and an inscription on the façade reads *Aux armées françaises et britanniques, l'empire britannique reconnaissant* ("To the French and British armies, from the grateful British Empire").

The Thiepval Memorial.

The Ulster Division

On the first day of the battle the 36th (Ulster) Division successfully managed to advance for about a mile; they had gained an advantage by not sticking to the rigid orders that had been issued. But unfortunately, owing to the difficulty of supplying ammunition, equipment, food and water to the men in forward positions and to the threat of German counter-attacks, it was feared that the forward Irish troops might be cut off and the decision was made to withdraw.

The Ulster Tower.

3 You leave the site towards the church to continue your route. At the crossroads you will see the Ulster Tower, a memorial for the 36th Division, on your left. It is about 900m out of your way but is well worth a visit.

◆ The Memorial Tower is a replica of the well-known Helen's Tower in Northern Ireland, which was located in the centre of the training camp where the volunteer Ulstermen of the 36th Division began their training before sailing to France.

Pozières

The ridge on which Pozières stands is the highest point in the Somme and the cornerstone of the German defences. The fortified village was an outpost to the second German defensive line and formed the centre of what was the British sector of the Somme.

After a preliminary artillery bombardment the 1st Australian Division attacked the German trenches on the western edge of the village and managed to capture a large enemy bunker known as Gibraltar and the only structure that was left standing. On 23 July an Australian brigade occupied the village and secured its position on the plateau.

The obelisk

The Battle of Pozières saw the first offensive action by Australian troops in the Somme, and although the battle is mostly remembered as an Australian victory, the cost was extremely high, with 5,285 fatalities for the 1st Australian Division, almost as many as the 5th had suffered in Fromelles just three day earlier. The tragic events of July 1916 are remembered throughout Australia. Around 50m from the remains of the bunker, a wooden platform offers a panoramic view over the fields between Thiepval and Pozières. When the sun is out, you can see the light reflecting off the Golden Virgin in Albert.

The 1st Australian Division Memorial.

❹ From Thiepval church the D73 takes you to the 1st Australian Division Memorial in Pozières and the adjacent remains of a large German bunker known as Gibraltar.

❺ From the obelisk, head for the busy D929 and ride 1.3km to the Tank Memorial at the foot of the radio mast with satellite dishes. Just opposite is the "Windmill".

The Tank Memorial.

The Windmill

Although the outpost had been captured, the main belt of German defence still had to be taken. At the other end of the village, on the road to Bapaume, before the war there was a windmill. This German concrete reinforced position was therefore indicated on the maps as "The Windmill". The 2nd Australian Division captured this position after bitter fighting and the loss of 6,848 men. In six weeks the Australians had lost more men in the Somme than over the eight months spent fighting in the Dardanelles. Remains of the windmill and the German blockhouse have been left and grassed over, leaving the undulating ground as a preserved battlefield site here.

◆ It was near this location that tanks first went into action, used by the British army as a new surprise weapon against the German army in the First World War on 15 September 1916.

6 Return to the D929 and turn left, where you will see the sign for the D73. Keep going until you can turn right onto the D20. After around 350m, turn left along the country road to Flatiron Copse Cemetery.

The two Philby brothers are buried side by side, followed by their service number (plot 1, row D, graves 35 and 36). Two more sets of two brothers are buried in this cemetery.

The 38th or Welsh Division

British Prime Minister Lloyd George persuaded Kitchener, Secretary of State for War, to raise a Welsh division. The 38th Division was formed in December 1914; it comprised battalions from Wales and was often known as the Welsh or Lloyd George's Division. From 3 to 12 July the division attacked Mametz Wood several times and by the time the wood had effectively been cleared of German resistance the division had lost 4,000 men. Facing the wood stands the Red Dragon, the memorial to the 38th Division, looking across the fields at the southern end of Mametz Wood. The barbed wire in its claws symbolises the fierce fighting against an enemy that was reluctant to give any ground.

The Red Dragon.

David Lloyd George

Before the war, David Lloyd George was a staunch pacifist and was considered to be an opponent of war, but when Belgium was invaded he supported Britain's entry into the First World War. He became Prime Minister in 1916 and called on the British people to support the war effort, stating that the war was too serious to be left to the military. During the military crisis in the spring of 1918 he agreed to the appointment of French General Foch as Commander-in-Chief on the Western Front. At the end of the war his reputation stood at an all-time high. He was seen as the man who won the war and was re-elected for the 1918-1922 term.

7 The road here becomes a dirt track for 800m until you reach the roundabout at the foot of the Welsh Memorial.

8 The pavement is now smooth all the way to the village of Mametz, where you take the D147 to Fricourt and bypass the D938. 500m north of Fricourt is the second-largest German military cemetery in the Somme in terms of numbers of graves, with 17,027. In 1920 the French authorities exhumed and added to this cemetery in Fricourt the German burials from 79 neighbouring villages in the valley of the Ancre and around Albert. Among the many Germans the remains of Manfred von Richthofen were transferred to this cemetery in 1925.

The Red Baron

With more than 80 official air combat victories, German fighter pilot Manfred von Richthofen is considered the top flying ace of the war. On 23 November 1916 Richthofen downed his most famous adversary, British ace Major Lanoe Hawker VC (see stage 6). In April 1918 he was fatally wounded but managed to make a controlled landing in the sector of the Australians, who buried him with full military honours. The French later exhumed him, as they did with so many other Germans, and transferred his remains to the large cemetery at Fricourt, where he was reinterred. In 1925 his youngest brother asked if the family could repatriate him.

The last journey of the Red Baron

With the authorisation of the French, his body was recovered and taken home to Germany to be laid to rest next to his brother Lothar. The German Government requested, however, that his final resting place be the *Invalidenfriedhof* in Berlin, where Richthofen received a state funeral. During the Cold War, the *Invalidenfriedhof* was on the boundary of the Soviet zone in Berlin. In 1975, with Soviet permission, his remains were moved to a family plot at the *Südfriedhof* in Wiesbaden, where he was buried for the fourth time next to his brother Bolko, his sister Elisabeth and her husband. Today in Berlin there is a marker where he was once buried.

The Cairn & "McCrae's Battalion".

9 2.5km further along the D147, immediately left of the village church of Contalmaison, is the Scottish monument. The advance from the British line in front of Albert was led by the 34th Division, a New Army formation recruited in Edinburgh, Northumberland, Grimsby and Cambridge. Elements of the 16th Royal Scots ("McCrae's Battalion") succeeded in penetrating the village defences on 1 July before being outnumbered and forced to withdraw by stubborn German opposition. The "Contalmaison Cairn" was unveiled in November 2004, completing a project first proposed by veterans of the battalion in 1919.

⑩ Back on the D20 in Contalmaison, you ride an easy 3km to La Boiselle. Turn left at a tea room and left again at the fork in a cul-de-sac where you see a sign for *La Grande Mine*. 1km along that street you will discover the most famous crater on the Western Front. On *Rue Georges Cuvillier* you will notice a tea room with an interesting name which is well worth a visit (www.oldblighty-somme.com).

◆ The high ground at La Boiselle was another objective of the first day of the Battle of the Somme. In order to breach the enemy's defences, Welsh miners dug a tunnel with a gallery that went under

Shell holes at the crater.

the German front. 27 tons of explosives blew a crater 100m wide and 30m deep and formed the start of the British infantry assault. Today this is a place of quiet meditation and every year on 1 July a short ceremony is held here to commemorate the battle.

◆ On 31 October 1998, British tourists walking around the rim of the crater discovered the remains of a soldier who was identified as Private George Nugent, serving with the 22nd Battalion Northumberland Fusiliers (Tyneside Scottish). Since 1 July 1916 he had been listed as missing in action but now has a known grave in Ovillers Military Cemetery. A wooden cross marks the place where he was found.

◆ The road back to Albert goes via Bécourt, where you take the *Rue d'Albert*.

Special Outing 2

From Pozières to Arras

The second stage of the Battle of the Somme

42km

There are two reasons for this Special Outing that forks off from the Remembrance Trail (stage 8). Firstly, it links Albert to Arras on new roads, giving cyclists an interesting 100km centre-based ride between the towns of Arras and Albert. And secondly, a visit to the Wellington Quarry is a must for anyone interested in the history of the Great War. The route also contains some less well-known sites that are particularly fascinating.

The Wellington Quarry and Memorial to the Battle of Arras.

❶ In Pozières, take the D73 towards Bazentin and after 1.3km turn left into a country road that leads to Martinpuich and an old German bunker.

❷ In Martinpuich, the D6 (later D107) passes an impressive military cemetery. 1.1km further on you turn left and then left again after another 660m. The white stone obelisk testifies to the local victory of the New Zealand Division that was in action here on 15 September 1916. Its objective was to breach the third German defence and create a gap for the cavalry to charge and capture Bapaume, an enemy logistical centre behind the lines.

The New Zealand Division in the Somme.

❸ Flers, 2.3km further on, was captured by the 41st Division and in the village a splendid monument to the 41st Division was erected. An identical statue stands in London.

❹ A short round trip from Flers to Gueudecourt gives you a chance to visit the Newfoundland trench and Caribou, which are well signposted.

❺ From Ligny-Thilloy your journey goes via Grévillers on the D10E1. Should you want a break or a rest or need to buy food or drinks, however, you can start by riding to Bapaume, which is a 2.7km direct ride on the D10.

A soldier in combat gear, ready to charge.

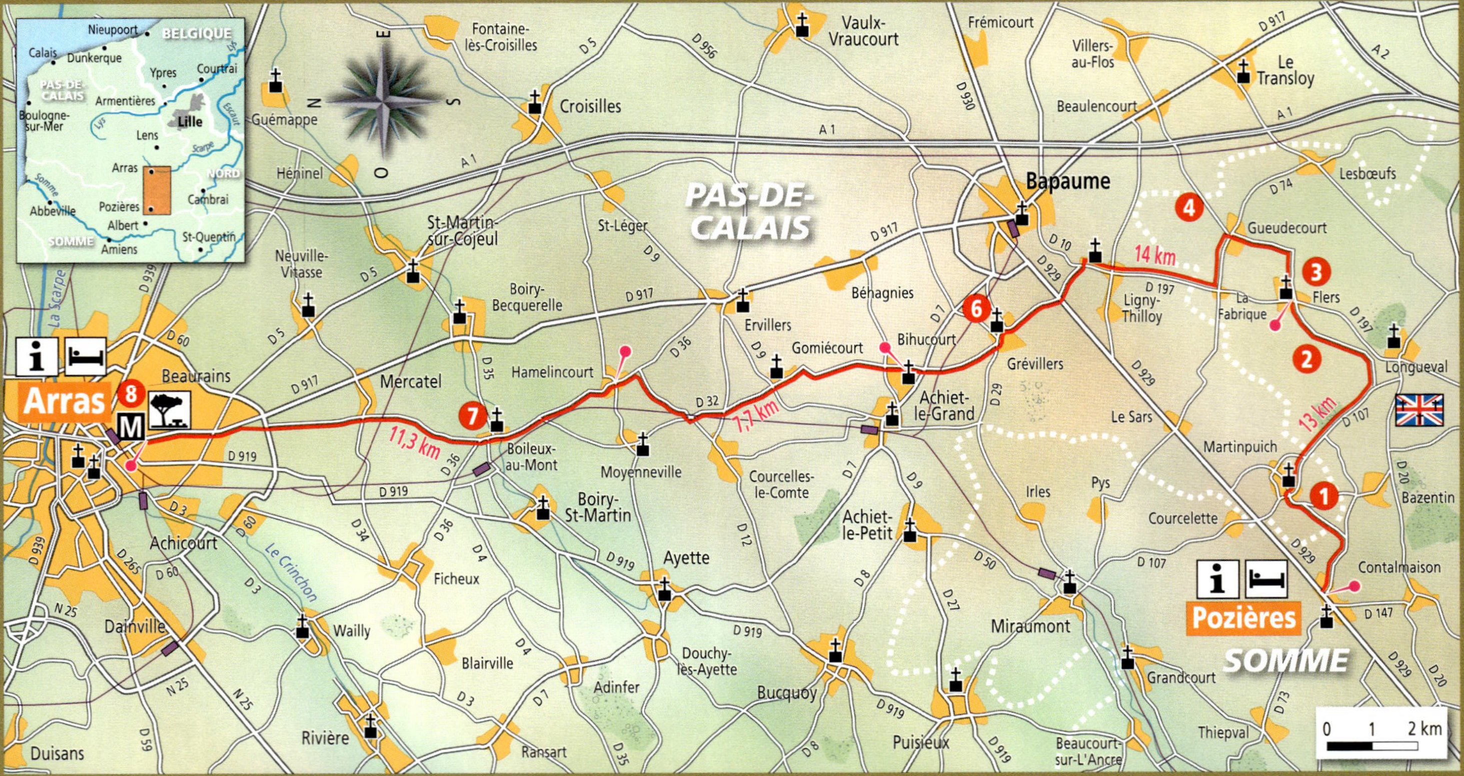

Arras
Pozières
PAS-DE-CALAIS
SOMME
Bapaume
11,3 km
7,7 km
14 km
13 km
1
2
3
4
6
7
8
Nieuport
BELGIQUE
Calais
Dunkerque
Ypres
Courtrai
Armentières
Lille
Boulogne-sur-Mer
Lens
Arras
NORD
Pozières
Cambrai
Abbeville
Albert
SOMME
Amiens
St-Quentin
Beaurains
Achicourt
Dainville
Duisans
Mercatel
Hamelincourt
Boileux-au-Mont
Boiry-St-Martin
Boiry-Becquerelle
St-Martin-sur-Cojeul
Neuville-Vitasse
Héninel
Guémappe
Croisilles
Fontaine-lès-Croisilles
St-Léger
Moyenneville
Ervillers
Gomiécourt
Béhagnies
Bihucourt
Achiet-le-Grand
Achiet-le-Petit
Courcelles-le-Comte
Ayette
Douchy-lès-Ayette
Adinfer
Ficheux
Wailly
Blairville
Rivière
Ransart
Bucquoy
Puisieux
Miraumont
Grévillers
Irles
Pys
Le Sars
Courcelette
Martinpuich
Ligny-Thilloy
La Fabrique
Flers
Gueudecourt
Lesbœufs
Le Transloy
Beaulencourt
Villers-au-Flos
Frémicourt
Vaulx-Vraucourt
Longueval
Bazentin
Contalmaison
Grandcourt
Thiepval
Beaucourt-sur-L'Ancre
Le Crinchon
La Scarpe
A 1
A 2
0 1 2 km

6 Cross the D929 to the village of Grévillers. Just outside the village lies one of the seven New Zealand Memorials to the Missing.

◆ From Grévillers, ride to Bihucourt, where you join the D7 for 260m before turning onto the D31 on your right. At the turn in the road you leave the D31 and join *Rue Neuve* towards Gomiécourt.

◆ After a very short stretch on the D9, turn left to Hamelincourt where you take the D36 to Boisleux.

7 In Boisleux you do not need to use any departmental roads; instead take the *Rue de la Mairie* towards Mercatel. In Mercatel, continue straight ahead on *Rue d'Arras*, the underpass of the busy D60, and you will arrive in Arras.

8 Turn left into *Rue Pierre Curie* and ride for 2.3km. The cycle path on *Rue de Bapaume* offers a safe ride to the centre. A little after the traffic lights there is a large supermarket, and just before the supermarket you will see the entrance to the park where you can visit the Wellington Quarry and Museum.

◆ Leave the Wellington Quarry and head for Arras along Avenue Fernand Lobbedez and the bridge over the railway.

The Wellington Quarry

The museum was set up in memory of the thousands of Commonwealth soldiers who lived under the town in the build-up to the Third Battle of Arras in 1917. It particularly commemorates the work of the New Zealand Tunnelling Company because this was their base. This is an underground museum in a section of the vast network of tunnels towards enemy lines that was created under the city. The guided tour takes over an hour and the museum closes at lunchtimes. It's best to enquire at the desk and find out when you can book your visit. The museum grounds are a good place for a picnic, with benches and good toilet facilities.

***Special Outing* 3**

From Pozières to Péronne

The French sector of the 1916 Battle of the Somme

26km

Like the previous outing, there are two reasons behind this route: it forks off and extends the Remembrance Trail from the British sector to the French sector in the Somme and also explores more historical sites from the 1916 Battle of the Somme.

Cyclists can use the link to Péronne to create a 100km-long centre-based loop between Albert and Péronne or an even longer loop from Péronne to Cambrai, Arras and Albert.

Delville Wood and the South African Memorial.

1 From Pozières, take the D73 to Bazentin, then turn left onto the D20 towards Longueval.

2 At the junction of the D20 and D197, a statue was erected in 2002 to commemorate the pipers who fell in all units in WWI. Many pipers continued to play despite wounds or a storm of bullets and shells falling around them, inspiring courage in the infantrymen.

Caterpillar Valley Cemetery

Caterpillar Valley is the second largest Commonwealth cemetery in the Somme. Its location, on the second German line, is interesting. From the wall at the back of this cemetery one can easily imagine the commanding views over the village of Montauban, Bernafay Wood and Trones Wood during the Allied offensive. From the gate at the entrance the New Zealand obelisk makes a distinctive feature on the horizon (north, see Special Outing 2). The screen wall is one of the seven New Zealand Memorials to the Missing. In 2004 the remains of an unknown New Zealand soldier were exhumed here for a last journey across the world to New Zealand.

An unknown New Zealand soldier rested here for 86 years; plot 14, row A, grave 27.

The Piper.

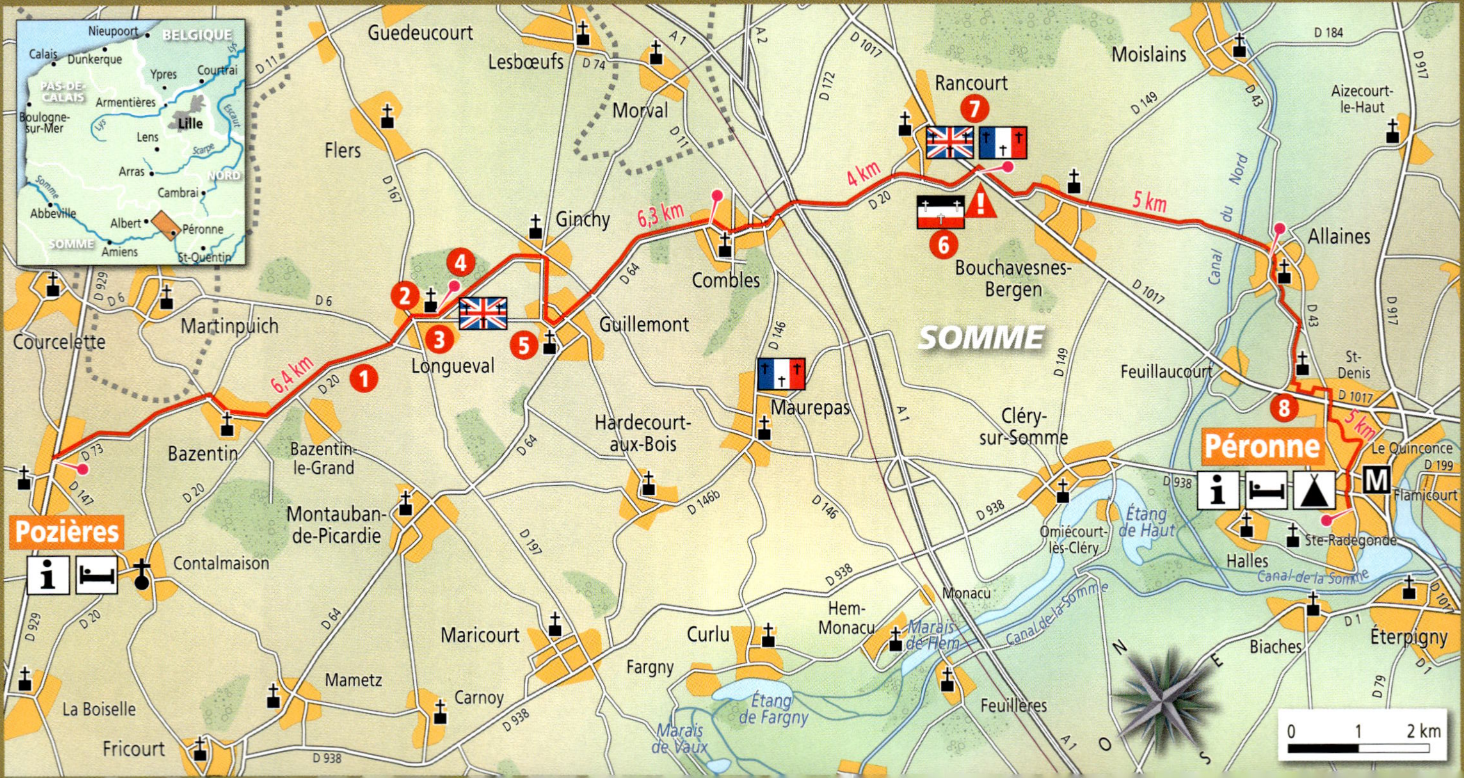
Pozières
Courcelette
Martinpuich
Bazentin
Bazentin-le-Grand
Contalmaison
La Boiselle
Fricourt
Mametz
Carnoy
Montauban-de-Picardie
Maricourt
Longueval
Flers
Guedeucourt
Lesbœufs
Morval
Ginchy
Guillemont
Hardecourt-aux-Bois
Combles
Maurepas
Curlu
Fargny
Hem-Monacu
Monacu
Rancourt
Bouchavesnes-Bergen
SOMME
Moislains
Allaines
Aizecourt-le-Haut
Feuillaucourt
Cléry-sur-Somme
Omiécourt-lès-Cléry
Feuillères
St-Denis
Péronne
Le Quinconce
Flamicourt
Ste-Radegonde
Halles
Biaches
Éterpigny
Étang de Haut
Étang de Fargny
Marais de Vaux
Marais de Flem
Canal de la Somme
Canal du Nord
6,4 km
6,3 km
4 km
5 km
5 km
1
2
3
4
5
6
7
8
D 73
D 147
D 929
D 6
D 20
D 167
D 11
D 74
A 1
A 2
D 1017
D 172
D 64
D 146
D 146b
D 197
D 938
D 149
D 43
D 184
D 917
D 199
D 1
D 79
0
1
2 km
N
E
S
O
Nieupoort
BELGIQUE
Calais
Dunkerque
Ypres
Courtrai
PAS-DE-CALAIS
Armentières
Boulogne-sur-Mer
Lille
Lens
Arras
NORD
Cambrai
Abbeville
Albert
Péronne
SOMME
Amiens
St-Quentin
Lys
Escaut
Scarpe
Somme

❸ 450m further along the D20, where the road to Ginchy forks off, the Memorial to the Footballers' Battalions was

inaugurated in 2010. Leading figures called on players to set an example in serving their country in its hour of need. The Conservative MP William Joynson-Hicks oversaw the creation of the 17th (1st Football) Battalion of the Middlesex Regiment. The battalion soon gained a full complement of recruits, though most were fans who liked the idea of serving with their footballing heroes. A second footballers' battalion was raised in June 1915.

❹ 250m along the road to Ginchy you will come to a large military cemetery and the South African National Memorial and Museum in Delville Wood. A double row of oak trees leads to the memorial. Behind the memorial is the museum, a pentagonal structure which houses four large bronze panels depicting the scenes of various wars and the participation of South Africa. Look out for the story of the Jackie, the mascot of the 3rd South African Infantry, in one of the frames on the wall.

The capture of Delville was an essential part of the offensive to take Flers and Bapaume (stage 2). The bronze panels tell how only 146 men out of 3,300 came out of the wood after six days of fighting.

Guillemont church is a significant site in Ireland's remembrance of the Great War.

5 Return to the road to Ginchy where, after 1.3km, you turn right to Guillemont and its church (on the main road), which is worth a visit. In September 1916 the fighting was particularly fierce here on the right flank of the British sector. It was for his brave action in this sector that Captain Noel Chavasse (stage 4) was awarded his first Victoria Cross.

Just left of the church is a memorial to the 16th (Irish) Division. This is essentially the same design, a Celtic cross, as the division's memorial in Wijtschate (stage 3)

6 Return to the D20 and ride to Combles and subsequently to Rancourt, a village which hosts British, French and German military cemeteries.

❼ Take a short round trip to the French *Chapelle du Souvenir* on the D1017 (N17) with the French military cemetery behind it and the British military cemetery on the opposite side of the road.

❽ Return to the D1017 for 850m, then turn left to ride parallel to the main road. Ride around the church of Bouchavesnes-Bergen and head up the *Route d'Allaines*. The last part of this stage will cost you some energy as you climb the Mont Saint-Quentin. Where you rejoin the D938 (formerly the N17), take care as the traffic can be busy. Turn right at the roundabout and at the next roundabout turn left and head downhill through quiet neighbourhoods to the centre of Péronne.

The Mont Saint-Quentin

This hilltop overlooking the Somme and the town of Péronne was another German stronghold and a cornerstone in their defences. If the French army did not succeed in capturing Péronne in 1916 it was because this hilltop remained under German control and frustrated every French attack. Early in September 1918 the 2nd Australian Division charged this position. Since they were severely under strength their commander ordered them to "scream like bushrangers" to make it seem like there were more of them. To their surprise the tactic worked, the enemy gave up its strategic position and the Somme was finally in Allied hands.

The 2nd Australian Division Memorial

Positioned at Mont Saint-Quentin, where the 2nd Australian Division captured one of the most formidable defensive positions on the Western Front, the 2nd Division's memorial was unconventional. Instead of an obelisk, the original memorial was a statue of an Australian soldier thrusting his bayonet into a German eagle sprawled at his feet. During the German occupation in 1940 their brigade removed and destroyed the statue, leaving only the stone plinth. In 1971 the new statue, showing an Australian soldier standing proud in full battle kit, was installed.

Stage 9

From Albert to Péronne

The 1918 offensive and counter-offensive in the Somme

84km

This stage follows the pace of the enemy's advance in the Somme during the 1918 German Saint Michael (Spring) Offensive to the point where they were checked and stopped before Amiens, at Villers-Bretonneux. From there you follow the retreat of the Germans as they fell back behind the Somme in Péronne (Mont Saint-Quentin) in September.

Since this is the longest of all the stages and is hilly over the full 84km, it would be wise to plan it well. The pretty town of Corbie, maybe combined with the Special Outing to Amiens, makes a perfect halfway stop on this long itinerary.

One of the prettiest crossings of the river Somme, at Omiécourt.

The German 1918 Spring Offensive

After the collapse of the Russian Empire, Soviet Russia and the Central Powers signed an armistice. This allowed Germany to move troops from the Eastern Front to the Western Front and launch a series of offensives in an attempt to win the war before the American forces built up strength. Operation Michael involved a vast push westwards from Saint-Quentin following the valley of the Somme towards Amiens. Using new infantry and artillery tactics, the Germans broke through on the front of the Fifth British Army and the boundary with the French army. Nothing seemed able to stop the enemy from advancing to Paris.

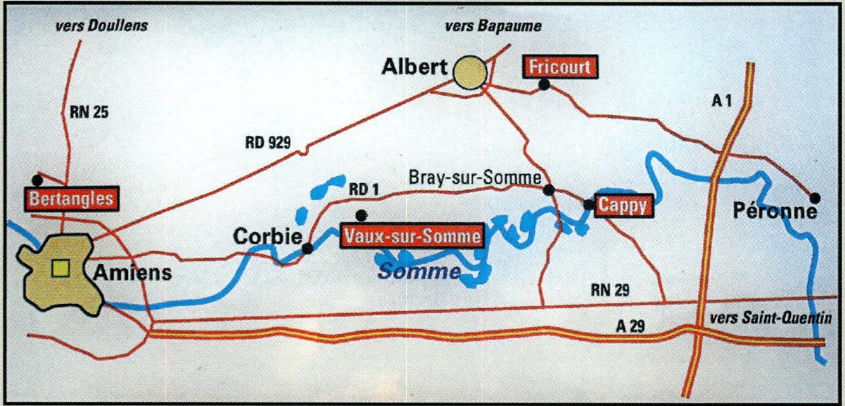

The Allies fall back in the Somme

When the Germans captured Albert, the British forces retreated to Amiens, the vital logistical railway centre supplying almost a million Allied soldiers. The British commanders considered a tactical retreat to the English Channel. The French wanted to save Paris. French Prime Minister Georges Clemenceau believed that the French Government should prepare to evacuate the capital and go to Bordeaux, but the President, Poincaré, refused to leave Paris. Under these circumstances the Allies decided to hold a conference in Compiègne and then Doullens, and General Foch was named Commander-in-Chief of the Allied Armies.

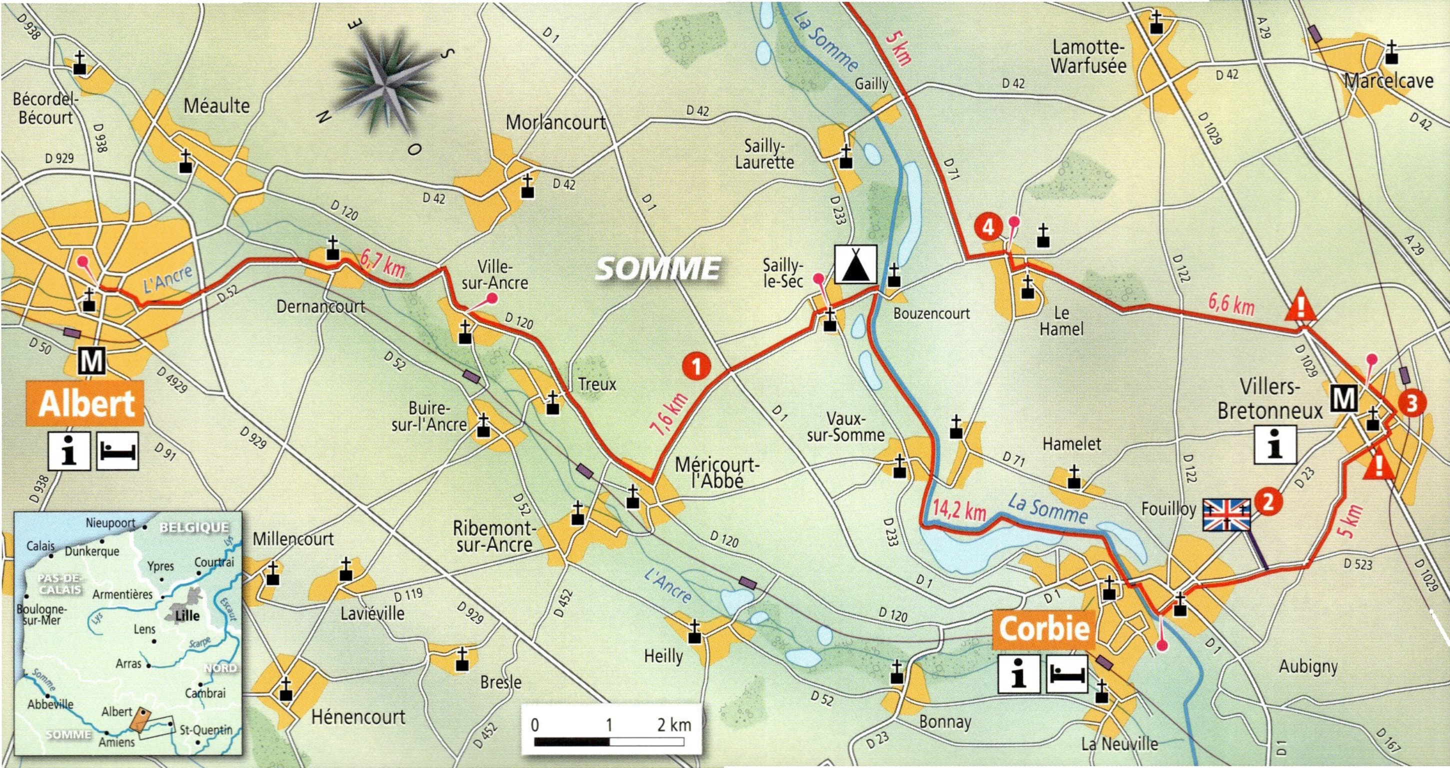

Albert
Méaulte
Bécordel-Bécourt
Morlancourt
Sailly-Laurette
Gailly
Lamotte-Warfusée
Marcelcave
Dernancourt
Ville-sur-Ancre
SOMME
Sailly-le-Sec
Bouzencourt
Le Hamel
Villers-Bretonneux
Treux
Buire-sur-l'Ancre
Vaux-sur-Somme
Méricourt-l'Abbé
Hamelet
Fouilloy
Ribemont-sur-Ancre
Millencourt
Laviéville
Heilly
Bresle
Hénencourt
Bonnay
Corbie
La Neuville
Aubigny
La Somme
L'Ancre
6,7 km
7,6 km
14,2 km
5 km
6,6 km
5 km
1
2
3
4
0
1
2 km
Nieupoort
BELGIQUE
Calais
Dunkerque
Ypres
Courtrai
PAS-DE-CALAIS
Armentières
Lille
Boulogne-sur-Mer
Lens
Arras
NORD
Cambrai
Abbeville
Albert
St-Quentin
SOMME
Amiens

The right man in the right place

It became clear that better coordination was needed between the Allies. They decided to meet to form a more unified command. General Ferdinand Foch was appointed Commander-in-Chief to manage all Allied operations. Georges Clemenceau justified his decision with the following words: "If we have to die, at least we will die fighting!" Foch was a good tactician with a good understanding of the spirit of the different armies. He successfully coordinated the efforts of all parties to save Amiens, the link between the French and British armies and the base for the next phase.

❶ The ninth stage starts in Albert. Take the D52 and ride 4km to Dernancourt, where you turn left and immediately right in front of the church. 1.9km further on, at the junction with the D120, turn right and follow the valley of the Ancre river all the way to Méricourt. It makes a sharp turn into *Rue Sailly-le-Sec* in Méricourt, where you leave the bank of the river to climb Morlancourt Ridge.

◆ At the crossroads stands the 3rd Australian Division Memorial. On this very spot the German advance was brought to a halt on the north bank of the Somme.

The Australian Memorial.

❷ Go straight on from the memorial and ride downhill to the valley of the Somme. In Sailly, cross the D233 and ride straight on to the river and the towpath that has recently become a cycle path. After 7km you will come to Corbie, where you cross the river and make your way to the south bank of the Somme and the Australian Memorial.

The Australian Memorial was inaugurated in 1938.

◆ Every year on 25 April, thousands gather here at the foot of this tower for a dawn service to commemorate this defining moment in Australian history. In Australia and New Zealand 25 April is known as Anzac Day.

❸ From the memorial, return to the route and climb 2km to Villers-Bretonneux, where you carefully cross the D1029 to the town hall and follow the signs for Victoria School.

Victoria School.

◆ From 1923 to 1927, the school in Villers-Bretonneux was rebuilt using donations from school children in Victoria. In the playground and above every blackboard is the inscription *N'oublions jamais l'Australie* ("Let us never forget Australia"). Also situated in the school is Victoria Hall, with its wooden panelling. On the first floor is the Franco-Australian Museum (www.museeaustralien.com).

The Battle of Villers-Bretonneux

On 24 April at 6:00am the Germans struck Villers-Bretonneux and by 10:00am they had taken the village, further consolidating their position during the day.
English and Australian units were ordered to recapture the village and the counter-attack started during the night of 24-25 April. Two Australian brigades swept around the village and met, surrounding the Germans and regaining the village.
This was not the largest battle fought in the war but it marked a turning point, putting an end to the German advance in the Somme.

4 Don't return to the town hall after your visit but ride straight onto *Rue Driot*. At the roundabout turn onto *Rue du Hamel* so that you can avoid the busy D1029. Navigate the roundabout carefully, and once that is behind you the 5km ride to Le Hamel is a delight! When you arrive in Le Hamel, turn right and go left behind the big red brick farmhouse. Just 25m further on, turn again and follow the signs for the Australian Memorial.

5 Return to the road and ride along the D71 to Cerisy, enjoying the panoramic views over the Somme valley. Cross the river in Chipilly.

The Battle of Le Hamel

The strategy, preparations, training, coordination and execution of every single element were so well orchestrated that the objective to capture the hilltop in 92 minutes was indeed achieved. Australian commander John Monash proved that the stalemate could be ended. This strategy was repeated on a much larger scale on 8 August in the Battle of Amiens, considered to be the turning point of the war. Some 800 American soldiers joined the Australians for the attack and Monash confirmed 4 July, US Independence Day, as the date for the battle to take place. This brought the Australian front on the south bank of the Somme in line with the line on the north bank (Sailly).

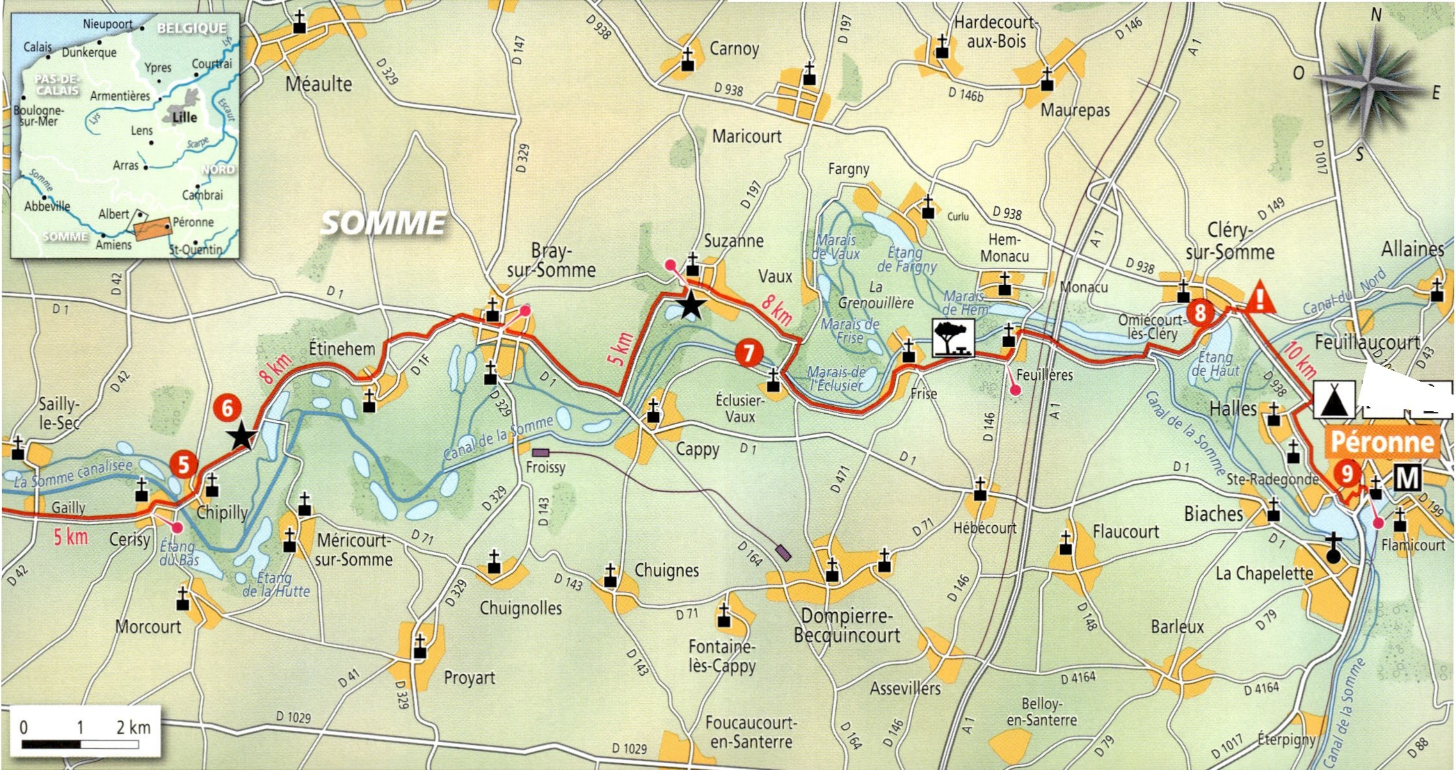

SOMME
Méaulte
Carnoy
Hardecourt-aux-Bois
Maurepas
Maricourt
Fargny
Curlu
Hem-Monacu
Monacu
Cléry-sur-Somme
Allaines
Feuillaucourt
Péronne
Bray-sur-Somme
Suzanne
Vaux
Étinehem
Sailly-le-Sec
Gailly
Cerisy
Chipilly
Méricourt-sur-Somme
Morcourt
Chuignolles
Proyart
Chuignes
Fontaine-lès-Cappy
Foucaucourt-en-Santerre
Cappy
Froissy
Éclusier-Vaux
Frise
Feuillères
Hébécourt
Dompierre-Becquincourt
Assevillers
Belloy-en-Santerre
Flaucourt
Barleux
Biaches
La Chapelette
Ste-Radegonde
Halles
Omiécourt-lès-Cléry
Flamicourt
Éterpigny
La Grenouillère
Marais de Vaux
Étang de Fargny
Marais de Hem
Marais de Frise
Marais de l'Éclusier
Étang de Haut
Étang du Bas
Étang de la Hutte
La Somme canalisée
Canal de la Somme
Canal du Nord
5 km
8 km
5 km
8 km
10 km
5
6
7
8
9
M
N
O
E
S
D 1
D 1F
D 42
D 41
D 71
D 79
D 88
D 143
D 146
D 146b
D 147
D 148
D 149
D 164
D 197
D 199
D 329
D 471
D 938
D 1017
D 1029
D 4164
D 43
A 1
0
1
2 km
Calais
Nieupoort
Dunkerque
BELGIQUE
PAS-DE-CALAIS
Ypres
Courtrai
Armentières
Boulogne-sur-Mer
Lille
Lys
Escaut
Lens
Scarpe
Arras
NORD
Somme
Cambrai
Abbeville
Albert
Péronne
SOMME
Amiens
St-Quentin

The 58th Division Memorial

In a little square opposite the church sits one of the most moving memorials. It is dedicated to those who died while fighting with the 58th (London) Division, including during the Battle of Amiens in August 1918, but it is better known as the statue that depicts an artilleryman cradling the head of his wounded horse. This divisional memorial is unusual because it includes the figure of a war horse. The inclusion of the horse pays tribute to the millions of horses who served alongside the military in the 1914-1918 war.

6 Prepare for a stiff but short climb when you leave Chipilly for Etinehem, but the physical effort is largely compensated by the wonderful panoramic view over the valley of the Somme. This viewpoint is a perfect place to take a break, enjoy the view and eat a snack in the picnic area. Before you continue your journey it is wise to test your brakes before you start to race downhill.

7 In Etinehem, follow the D1 to Bray-sur-Somme, where you have to watch out for traffic as you continue on the D1 to Cappy. Do not cross the river at Cappy but turn left onto the D197 to Suzanne. The history of the château is told on a plaque on the opposite side of the gate. The crossing of the Somme at Eclusier-Vaux is considered to be the most beautiful of all the river crossings.

8 You now come to a flat stretch along the bank of the Somme to Frise and Feuillères. Follow the river for 10km and cross it again at Omiécourt.

Panoramic view in Chipilly.

9 For a short time you have to ride along the busy D938 to make your way to Péronne. You have to wait until you cross the bridge over the canal to find an alternative road. The little road to Halle leads to the gardens behind the château and museum of Péronne.

The castle and museum.

Péronne – twice occupied and destroyed

On their way to Paris, the German armies captured Péronne and had the population evacuate their town. Many went to Switzerland under the care of the Red Cross and stayed in refugee camps. In 1917, when the Germans fell back on their newly constructed defence line known as the Hindenburg Line, the people returned and started to rebuild. But in the spring of 1918 the Germans retook the town and the population was evacuated for the second time. When they returned after September 1918 they found their town and homes totally destroyed again.

◆ The old gate between the two mediaeval towers forms the entrance to the *Historial de la Grande Guerre* museum. All the information is in three languages: French, English and German. The museum presents the experiences of the main participants in the First World War and the impact this conflict had on the 20th century (www.historial.org).

◆ The rebuilt town hall also hosts the Alfred Danicourt archaeological museum. 95% of its collection was lost in the war. Only a few rare pieces could be saved by the curator, who buried them in the garden before the Germans occupied the city in August 1914.

The Town Hall.

Special Outing 4
From Corbie to Amiens
The railway centre for the Somme front

20km

This Special Outing links the town of Corbie to the city of Amiens, an important railway centre and the capital of Picardy. Combining this route with stage 9 links Amiens to Albert or Péronne and to all the historic sites in the Somme and beyond. So Amiens could well be your base or starting point for your bike trip. Corbie is a lovely town but cannot rival with Amiens in terms of monuments, museums, walks and art.

The towpath along the Somme.

1 Start your journey in the square in front of the church of Corbie and look for the post office to find the D30. The abbey church was once part of a much larger walled abbey and gardens, which formed an important cultural centre in the early Middle Ages.

Saint-Pierre abbey church.

2 1.2km after the D30 crosses over the railway, you come to the village of La Neuville and its church in Flamboyant Gothic style with a unique main entrance. This is one of the loveliest Gothic churches in all of Picardy.

3 Return to the D30 for just 180m before turning left into *Route de Daours* with its great view over the Somme. Once in Daours, take the D1 for 350m before turning left to ride on the quiet country roads between the D1 and the Somme to Lamotte-Brebière.

Corbie

Corbie suffered great damage during the artillery bombardments of 1918. After the war many French cities that hadn't been destroyed offered to help with the reconstruction of the devastated towns in the north and east of France. This town was adopted by the city of Chartres and received 45,000 francs. The old château is now the town hall and was entirely renovated in 2013, as was the public garden around it. A special *Espace Chartres* area was created and inaugurated to honour the city that helped it to rise from its ashes after the war.

Town Hall.

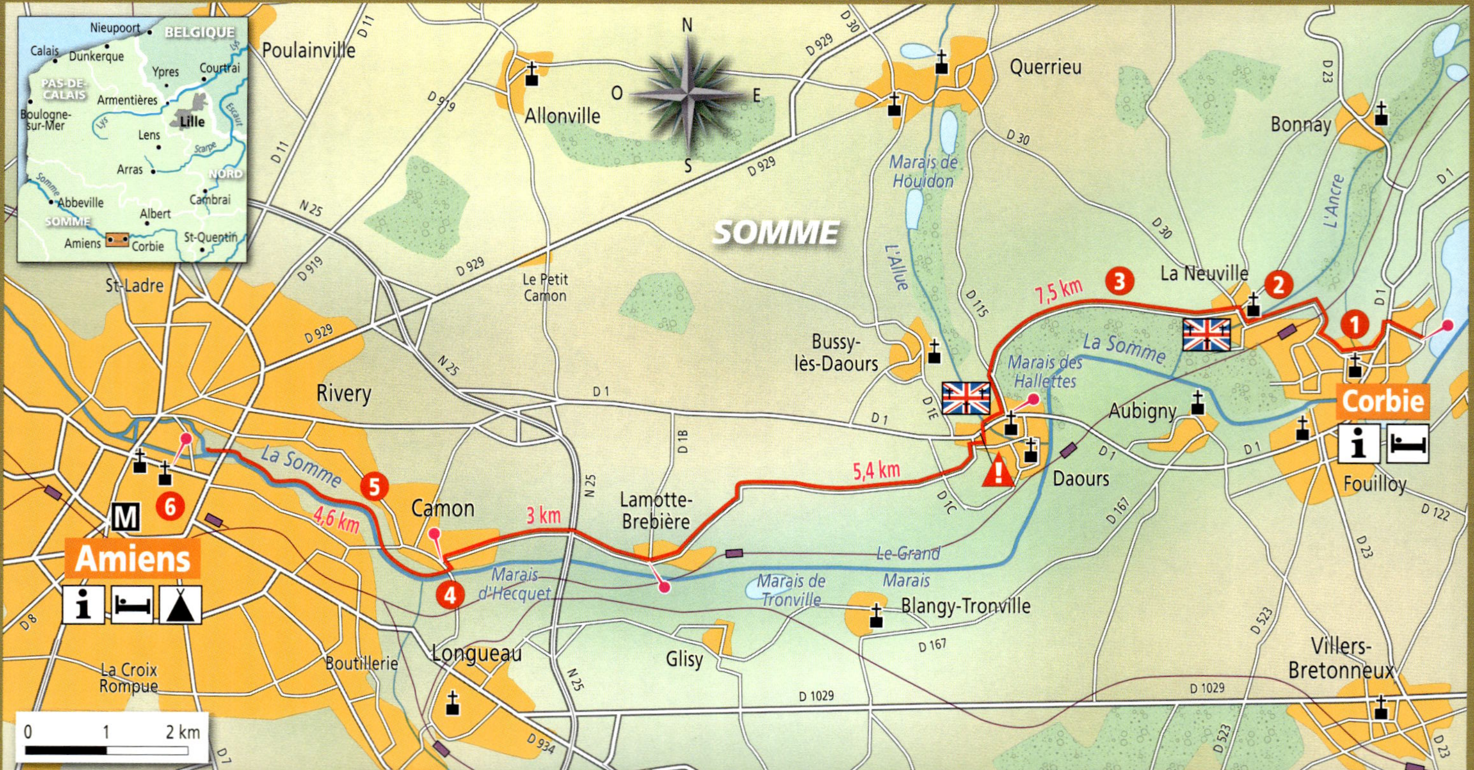

Corbie
Fouilloy
Villers-Bretonneux
Bonnay
La Neuville
Aubigny
Daours
Querrieu
Bussy-lès-Daours
Blangy-Tronville
Lamotte-Brebière
Glisy
Le Petit Camon
Allonville
Poulainville
Rivery
Camon
Longueau
Boutillerie
St-Ladre
La Croix Rompue
Amiens
SOMME
La Somme
L'Ancre
L'Allue
Marais de Houdon
Marais des Hallettes
Le Grand Marais
Marais de Tronville
Marais d'Hecquet
7,5 km
5,4 km
3 km
4,6 km
1
2
3
4
5
6
M
N
S
E
O
D 1
D 1E
D 1C
D 1B
D 23
D 30
D 115
D 122
D 167
D 523
D 929
D 919
D 11
D 1029
D 934
D 8
D 7
N 25
0
1
2 km
Nieuport
BELGIQUE
Calais
Dunkerque
Ypres
Courtrai
PAS-DE-CALAIS
Armentières
Boulogne-sur-Mer
Lille
Lys
Escaut
Lens
Scarpe
Arras
NORD
Somme
Abbeville
Cambrai
Albert
SOMME
Amiens
Corbie
St-Quentin

Hortillonnages

Floating gardens or hortillonnages are part of the natural habitat of the Somme valley. With numerous canals on the flat riverbed making the fertile gardens look like little islands, Amiens is sometimes known as the "Venice of the North".

Vegetable growing was once very important here but now the 300-hectare network of canals can be visited on flat boats that are powered by electric motors and give you the impression that you're floating on the water.

Here and there you can find a path into the hortillonnages.

④ In Lamotte-Brebière you ride parallel to the bank of the Somme but you only come to the tow-path (also open to walkers) just before you reach the village of Camon. Amiens is just a stone's throw away.

◆ After a short period of occupation by the enemy in 1914, Amiens became a vital logistical and hospital centre for the Allies in the northern part of the Western Front. As the city was situated well behind the lines, most of its population remained in place and the city was a bustling centre for English, Canadian, Australian, Indian and also French African troops.

The beautiful Gothic Cathedral of Amiens is a jewel in Picardy's cultural heritage.

Stage 10

From Péronne to Cambrai via Bony

The Hindenburg Line

65km

The first part of your itinerary follows the forced retreat of the Germans to the Hindenburg Line. The sector between Péronne and the Hindenburg Line didn't experience a stalemate as there was elsewhere in the Somme. Other than a handful of military cemeteries there are no impressive monuments or memorials like the ones in Thiepval or Vimy. As a result, this sector receives fewer visitors and remains somewhat forgotten, which is unjustified since the rapid series of Allied victories here brought the war to an end much sooner than the Germans or Allies expected. The second part of the itinerary follows the Saint-Quentin Canal all the way into Cambrai.

The Saint-Quentin Canal to Cambrai.

The first retreat behind the Hindenburg Line

After the Battle of the Somme and the Brusilov Offensive in Russia the Germans constructed a new line of defence between Arras and the Marne that was intended to counter fresh Anglo-French attacks in 1917 and shorten the defensive lines to prepared positions which would save on manpower. By destroying the roads and demolishing civilian buildings in the salient before their withdrawal, the Germans would force an Allied offensive into a zone which had been turned into a "desert". The retreat took place in February and March 1917. Several Allied attempts to breach the Hindenburg Line in 1917 failed (see Bullecourt, stage 11).

The second retreat behind the Hindenburg Line

The success of the Battle of Amiens on 8 August 1918 was largely due to the efficiency of the single Allied command and the use of a new Allied weapon: the tank. The enemy was forced to retreat and took position behind the Somme in Péronne. After losing Mont Saint-Quentin and Péronne the Germans withdrew behind the Hindenburg Line, cratering roads and ripping up all railways as part of a scorched-earth strategy. Their plan was now to sit out the winter and use that time to negotiate an "honourable" peace.

❶ Leave Péronne following the same route as the last part of stage 3. At *Avenue Charles de Gaulle*, climb up to Mont Saint-Quentin.

◆ Towards Allaines you can either stay on the D43 or take the scenic route along the slopes of Mont Saint-Quentin.

❷ Leave the D43 in Haut-Allaines and take the road to Aizecourt-le-Haut, where you cross the D917 and go downhill to Driencourt. From the D181, ride along the D101 in Longavesnes all the way to Ronssoy.

❸ In Ronssoy, stay on the D6 for just 250m before turning right into the *Rue du 14 Juillet*.

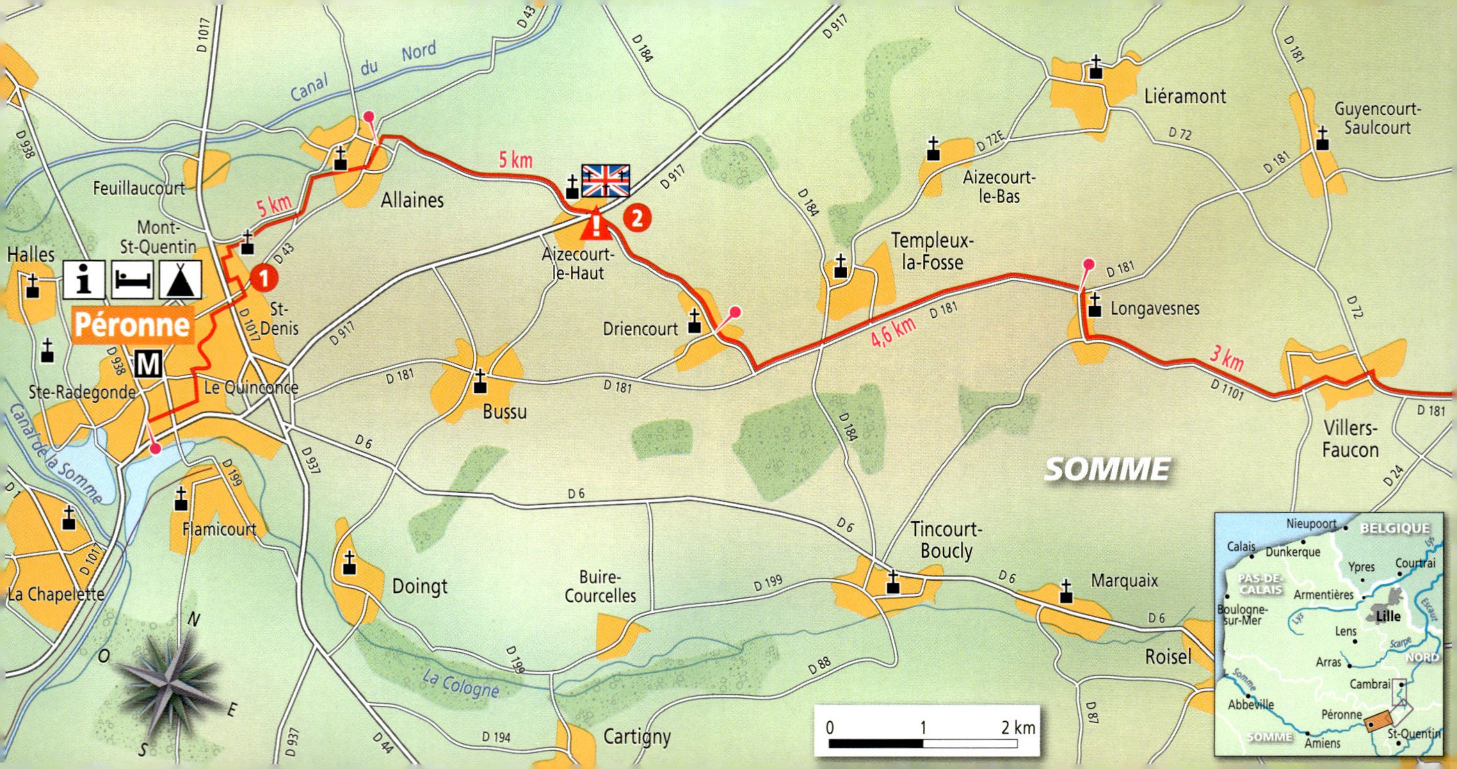

Péronne
Halles
Mont-St-Quentin
Feuillaucourt
Ste-Radegonde
Le Quinconce
St-Denis
Allaines
Aizecourt-le-Haut
Driencourt
Bussu
Templeux-la-Fosse
Aizecourt-le-Bas
Liéramont
Guyencourt-Saulcourt
Longavesnes
Villers-Faucon
Tincourt-Boucly
Marquaix
Roisel
Doingt
Buire-Courcelles
Cartigny
Flamicourt
La Chapelette
SOMME
Canal du Nord
Canal de la Somme
La Cologne
5 km
5 km
4,6 km
3 km
D 1017
D 43
D 917
D 184
D 181
D 72
D 72E
D 938
D 6
D 937
D 199
D 88
D 194
D 44
D 87
D 1101
D 24
0
1
2 km
N
E
S
O
Nieupoort
BELGIQUE
Calais
Dunkerque
Ypres
Courtrai
PAS-DE-CALAIS
Armentières
Lille
Boulogne-sur-Mer
Lens
Arras
NORD
Cambrai
Abbeville
Péronne
SOMME
Amiens
St-Quentin
Lys
Escaut
Scarpe
Somme

Objective: to breach the Hindenburg Line

Foch was convinced that victory could be won in 1918 if the enemy was not given time to settle in its prepared positions. He ordered the Commonwealth Armies to attack between Cambrai and Saint-Quentin, the Belgians in the north, the French south of Saint-Quentin and the Americans in the Saint-Mihiel Salient. This final period of the war is known as the Hundred Days' Offensive, and stages 10 and 11 will take you to some of the fields where these decisive battles took place.

4 Continue straight on for 3km before turning right towards Bony and the Somme American Cemetery. This is one of eight World War I American military cemeteries in France. The graves do not have headstones but instead white marble crosses or a Star of David. The names of the missing soldiers are engraved on the wall of the chapel. The superintendent's office has a hall and living room that is open to welcome visitors and offer a place to reflect or ask for information.

5 Return to the gate, take the road to Bony and go straight along the D442 towards the D1044. Around 500m after leaving the village behind you, you will see boats sailing under the road through a 6km-long tunnel. At the junction with the D1044 you ride straight on to *Le Mont Saint-Martin*.

The Somme American Cemetery.

6 When you reach *Le Mont Saint-Martin* (the D71), turn left to Le Catelet and head for the church and the little cemetery next to it.

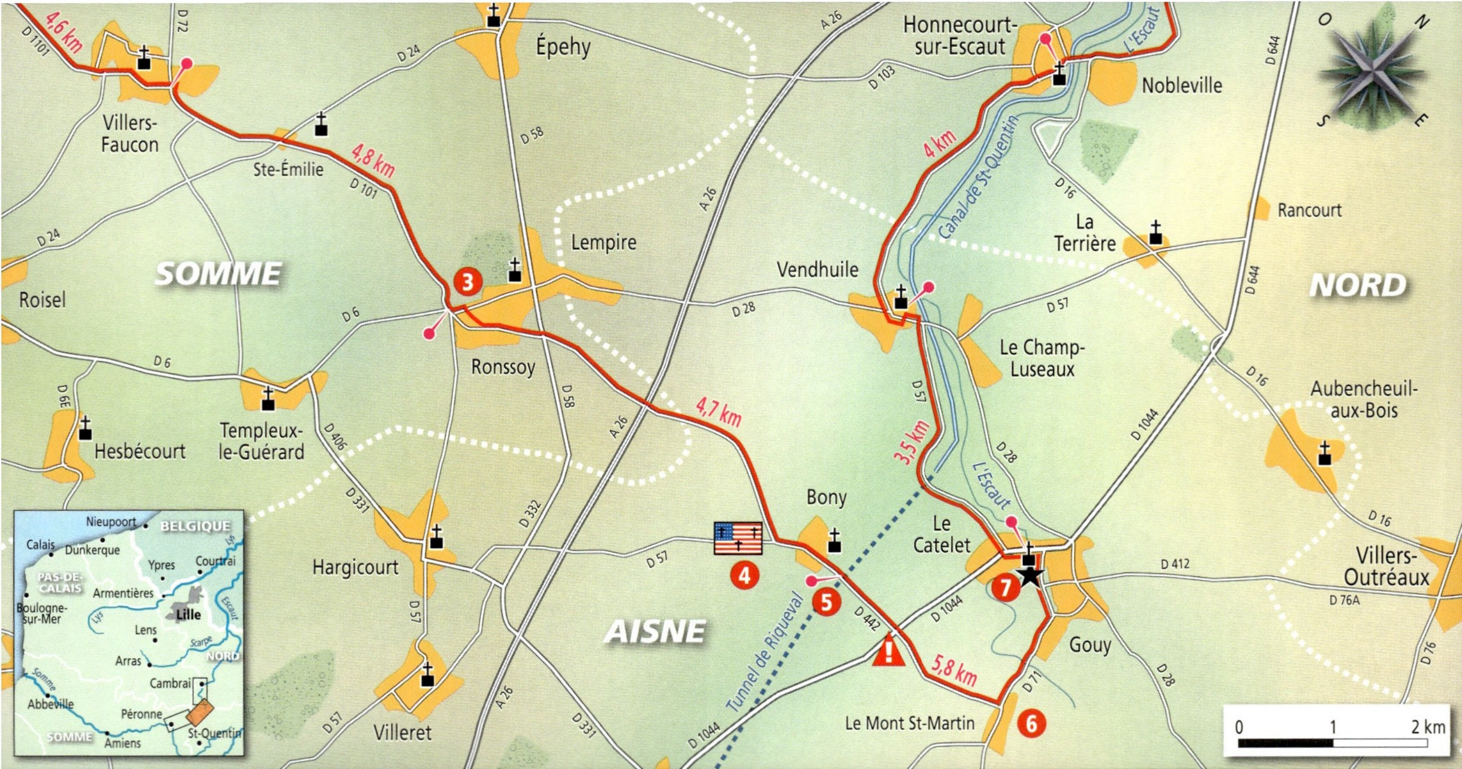
NORD
SOMME
AISNE
Honnecourt-sur-Escaut
Nobleville
Épehy
Villers-Faucon
Ste-Émilie
Lempire
Roisel
Ronssoy
Vendhuile
La Terrière
Rancourt
Le Champ-Luseaux
Aubencheuil-aux-Bois
Templeux-le-Guérard
Hesbécourt
Hargicourt
Villeret
Bony
Le Catelet
Gouy
Villers-Outréaux
Le Mont St-Martin
Canal-de-St-Quentin
L'Escaut
Tunnel de Riqueval
4,6 km
4,8 km
4,7 km
4 km
3,5 km
5,8 km
3
4
5
6
7
D 1101
D 72
D 24
D 58
D 101
D 6
D 6E
D 406
D 331
D 332
D 57
D 28
D 103
D 16
D 644
D 1044
D 442
D 412
D 76A
D 76
D 71
A 26
O
N
S
E
0
1
2 km
BELGIQUE
Nieupoort
Calais
Dunkerque
Ypres
Courtrai
PAS-DE-CALAIS
Armentières
Lille
Boulogne-sur-Mer
Lens
Lys
Escaut
Scarpe
NORD
Arras
Cambrai
Somme
Abbeville
Péronne
St-Quentin
SOMME
Amiens

The Saint-Quentin Canal

The canal was built in two phases, the second much longer than the first. The highest point of the Saint-Quentin Canal (84m) is situated between Lesdins and Vendhuile. Connecting the Seine Basin with the Escaut was a lengthy process that took two tunnels across limestone ridges, one "short" tunnel (1,098m long) and one long tunnel (5,670m long), which goes from Le Catelet to Riqueval. The Allied commanders saw the tunnel as a 6km-wide bridge across the canal and the only location for a massive infantry attack supported by tanks.

The Battle of Bellicourt

This spearhead attack against the Hindenburg Line involved British, American and Australian forces and is named after the village on top of the tunnel, Bellicourt. Owing to thick fog and poor coordination the inexperienced American units lost contact and the confusion led to chaos and heavy losses. When the British 46th Division, on the right flank, found a bridge that the Germans had forgotten to blow up, they held the bridge, crossed the canal and released pressure on the left flank of the 30th American Division. The assault achieved all its objectives, resulting in a full breach of the Hindenburg Line. Six weeks later the armistice was signed.

The American Monument at Bellicourt (on the D1044).

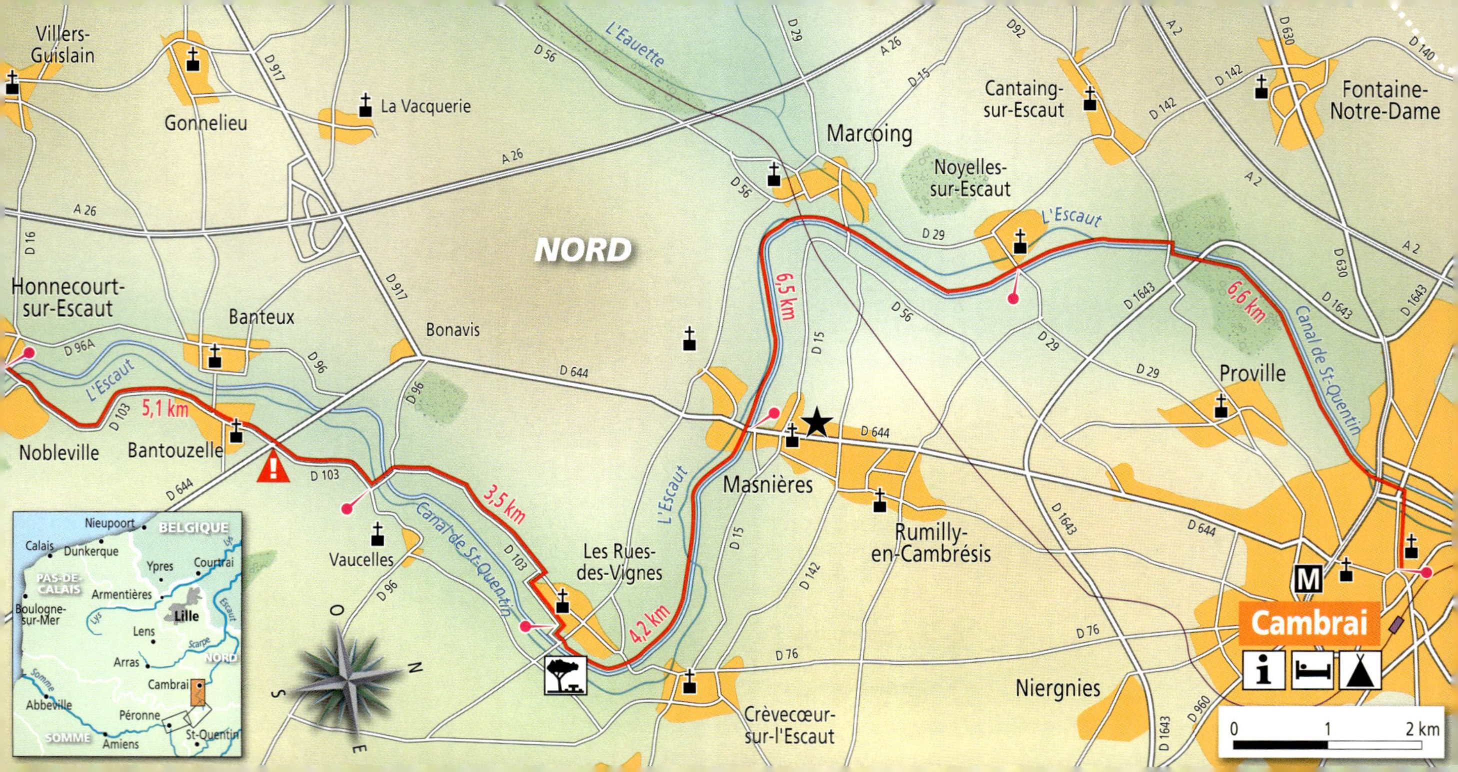
Villers-Guislain
Gonnelieu
La Vacquerie
Marcoing
Cantaing-sur-Escaut
Fontaine-Notre-Dame
Noyelles-sur-Escaut
L'Eauette
L'Escaut
NORD
Honnecourt-sur-Escaut
Banteux
Bonavis
Proville
6,5 km
6,6 km
Canal de St-Quentin
5,1 km
Nobleville
Bantouzelle
3,5 km
Masnières
Rumilly-en-Cambrésis
Vaucelles
Les Rues-des-Vignes
4,2 km
Crèvecœur-sur-l'Escaut
Niergnies
Cambrai
0
1
2 km
N
E
S
O
A 26
A 2
D 917
D 644
D 103
D 96
D 96A
D 56
D 29
D 15
D 142
D 1643
D 630
D 140
D 92
D 16
D 76
D 960
Nieupoort
BELGIQUE
Calais
Dunkerque
Ypres
Courtrai
PAS-DE-CALAIS
Armentières
Boulogne-sur-Mer
Lille
Lens
Arras
NORD
Cambrai
Abbeville
Péronne
SOMME
Amiens
St-Quentin
Escaut
Lys
Scarpe
Somme

7 At the church, ride along the D1044 to Saint-Quentin for 300m, then turn right onto the D440 and the D57 to Vendhuile. For 12.5km, follow local roads as you pass through the villages of Honnecourt, Bantouzelle and Vaucelles, before you reach the towpath along the canal. After passing a factory in Les Rues-des-Vignes, head for *Rue Basse*. A gap between houses on the right-hand side is a nice place to rest and to join the river bank. The next 18km are on the towpath and take you all the way to Cambrai.

The Paris Gate (Porte de Paris), the only remaining town gate.

The Englishman's Daughter

On 27 August 1914, four British soldiers became separated from their unit and isolated behind enemy lines. French country folk risked their lives to help them – the soldiers were taken in, given civilian clothes and told to blend in with the farming community. They lived right under the nose of the German occupier for sixteen months. One of those British soldiers, Robert Digby, fell in love with the most beautiful girl in Villeret, Claire Dessenne. The romance blossomed and it soon became apparent that she was pregnant. As the German occupiers tightened their grip on the French villagers' resources and freedoms, grumblings about the risks of hiding the fugitives began to surface among some of the people of Villeret. Someone betrayed the soldiers, who were subsequently executed as spies. When Robert's mother died, his brother found an old letter that revealed the existence of his niece in France. Ben Macintyre's book tells the moving story of the horror of occupation, the betrayal and how the girl, now a woman, met her uncle.

Robert Digby's headstone against the screen wall.

Special Outing 5
From Bony to Saint-Quentin
The Hindenburg Line breached

29km

The fifth Special Outing forks off at the American military cemetery in Bony and extends your journey along the Hindenburg Line towards the boundary of the British and French sectors in September 1918. This route follows the canal to the Somme river and symbolically links the American military cemetery to the French and German military cemeteries in Saint-Quentin. The valley of the Somme, the sector where the Fifth British Army was positioned on the outskirts of the town in March 1918, was the focus of the massive German offensive in the spring of 1918. The French liberated the town in October of that year.

An unusual haven of peace in the town of Saint-Quentin.

❶ Turn right upon leaving the American military cemetery and ride along the D57 before turning left at the junction with the D331 to Bellicourt. Within the English-speaking world, the tunnel is known as Bellicourt Tunnel, after the name of the village on top of the ridge. But the French know it as the tunnel of Riqueval. In Bellicourt, take the *Rue du Vieux Chemin* to Riqueval and cross over the D1044 (you don't have to ride on this busy road).

❷ The museum tells you the history of its construction, the tow boats and how Napoleon Bonaparte inaugurated it in 1810. Take the little country road behind the car park and ride along the canal until you reach the famous Riqueval Bridge.

The steep slopes where the bed of the canal cuts into the ridge.

Riqueval Bridge

The steep slopes of the 10m-wide canal were an integral part of the German defence system and formed a formidable physical obstacle to cross for most infantrymen who couldn't swim. Here the thick fog helped the 46th British Division because the Germans were not aware of their approach across the slopes. The one bridge that the enemy had used to supply their outposts on the Hindenburg Line was captured before they had time to blow it up. When this division breached the enemy's lines it released the right flank of the American 30th Division, who widened the gap, resulting in a total break in the Hindenburg Line. The 46th was credited with this victory and the brigade commander addressed his troops from this bridge.

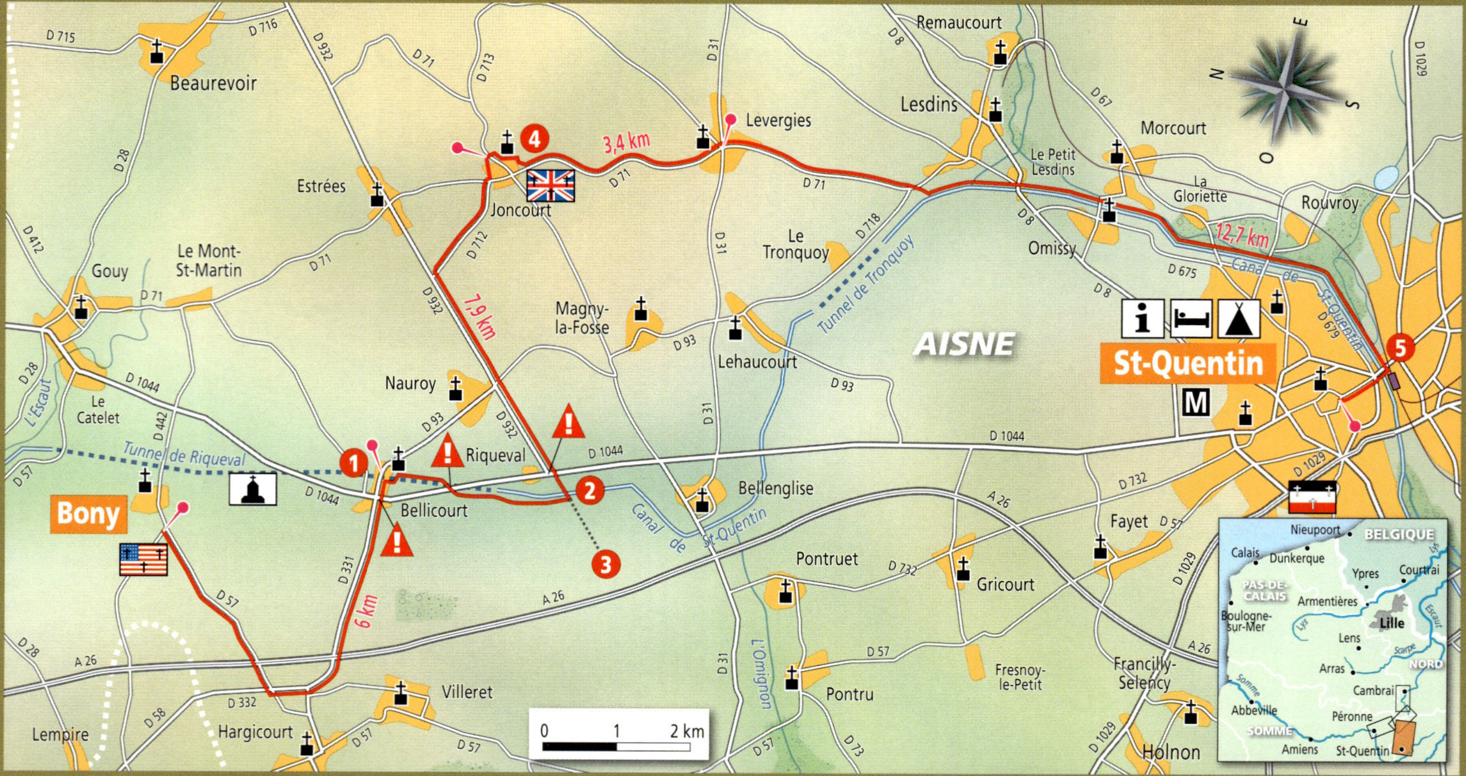
St-Quentin
AISNE
Bony
Beaurevoir
Estrées
Joncourt
Levergies
Lesdins
Remaucourt
Le Petit Lesdins
Morcourt
La Gloriette
Rouvroy
Omissy
Le Tronquoy
Magny-la-Fosse
Lehaucourt
Nauroy
Riqueval
Bellicourt
Bellenglise
Le Mont-St-Martin
Gouy
Le Catelet
Lempire
Hargicourt
Villeret
Pontruet
Pontru
Gricourt
Fresnoy-le-Petit
Fayet
Francilly-Selency
Holnon
Tunnel de Riqueval
Tunnel de Tronquoy
Canal de St-Quentin
L'Escaut
L'Omignon
3,4 km
7,9 km
6 km
12,7 km
1
2
3
4
5
0 1 2 km
D 715
D 716
D 932
D 71
D 713
D 31
D 8
D 67
D 1029
D 28
D 412
D 712
D 718
D 675
D 679
D 93
D 1044
D 442
D 57
D 331
D 332
D 58
A 26
D 732
D 73
BELGIQUE
Nieuwpoort
Calais
Dunkerque
Ypres
Courtrai
PAS-DE-CALAIS
Boulogne-sur-Mer
Armentières
Lille
Lens
Arras
NORD
Cambrai
Abbeville
Péronne
SOMME
Amiens
St-Quentin
Lys
Escaut
Scarpe
Somme

Memorial to the 4th Australian Division.

❸ A 2km-long grassy track leads to the 4th Australian Division Memorial. This division captured the former British reserve line that was overrun by the Germans during the March offensive, and the outpost line that screened the Hindenburg Line.

❹ Cross the D1044 and ride 3.3km along the D932 before turning right onto the D712.

◆ In Joncourt a message on the façade indicates that the US headquarters was posted here in October 1918. The villages here were not destroyed as the ones in the Somme were after years of stalemate and two offensives.

❺ Follow the D71 for 6km and at the junction with the D718 a very short gravel path takes you to the 7km-long towpath to Saint-Quentin station, with an interesting monument and two Art Deco posts designed as a lighthouse standing at the foot of the bridge.

◆ The semi-relief carvings are the work of Paul Landowski, a Polish/French monument sculptor. His best-known work is the Christ the Redeemer statue in Rio de Janeiro, Brazil. Here his work represents the different battles fought in and around the city.

Stage 11

From Cambrai to Arras

The Last Hundred Days

55km

This stage links the rivers Escaut and Scarpe and the towns of Cambrai and Arras. Stages 7, 8, 10 and 11 form a large loop and a long circular itinerary to the battlefields around six different French towns, returning you to where you started, left your vehicle or hired your bikes!

East of Cambrai you will see the marks of the violent combats in 1917 and 1918 to breach the Hindenburg Line. From Cantaing you will follow the old German line to Bullecourt. The last part of the stage is a gentle ride along the bank of the river Scarpe.

Strange encounters may be awaiting you along the towpath

❶ Leave Cambrai by the canal, the same way you arrived here for stage 10. After 5km, at the Cantaing sluice, leave the tow-path and take the D92 into the village. The cemetery indicates where the 51st Highland Division and British forces advanced deep behind the Hindenburg Line. This position was lost during the 1918 German counter-attack and recaptured during the last hundred days.

❷ After 2.2km on the D92, turn right to Bourlon.

❸ From Bourlon you ride to Sains-lès-Marquion. From Sains it's an easy 5.8km ride to Quéant on the D22. From Quéant, continue for 3.2km to Riencourt. In Riencourt, *Rue de Bullecourt* leads to the Australian memorial site

Cantaing Military Cemetery.

The first massive use of tanks at Cambrai

The failure of the Third Battle of Ypres pushed Haig to boost the morale of the troops and search for victory in other areas. In September he approved a plan for the massive use of tanks in an attempt to capture Cambrai, an important logistical centre for the German defences in this sector. The terrain was dry and perfect for the use of tanks. To break the Hindenburg Line 350 tanks were used on the first day and 476 in total. This was the largest number of tanks used in one single offensive. The objective of the attack over an 8km-wide front was to encircle and take Cambrai and the nearby Bourlon Ridge, which could be used to threaten the German line in the north.

The 1917 Battle of Cambrai

The first phase of the battle was a great success due to the element of surprise, careful preparation and effective artillery barrages ahead of the infantrymen and tanks in the field. But the lack of coordination, the excessive distance between tanks and infantry and the new German infiltration tactics and anti-tank training resulted in a British withdrawal. Bourlon Wood was also lost in the German counter-offensive. The British attack demonstrated that the Hindenburg Line could be penetrated and showed the value of new artillery and infantry methods. The German infiltration tactics proved to be an effective means of (re) capturing ground.

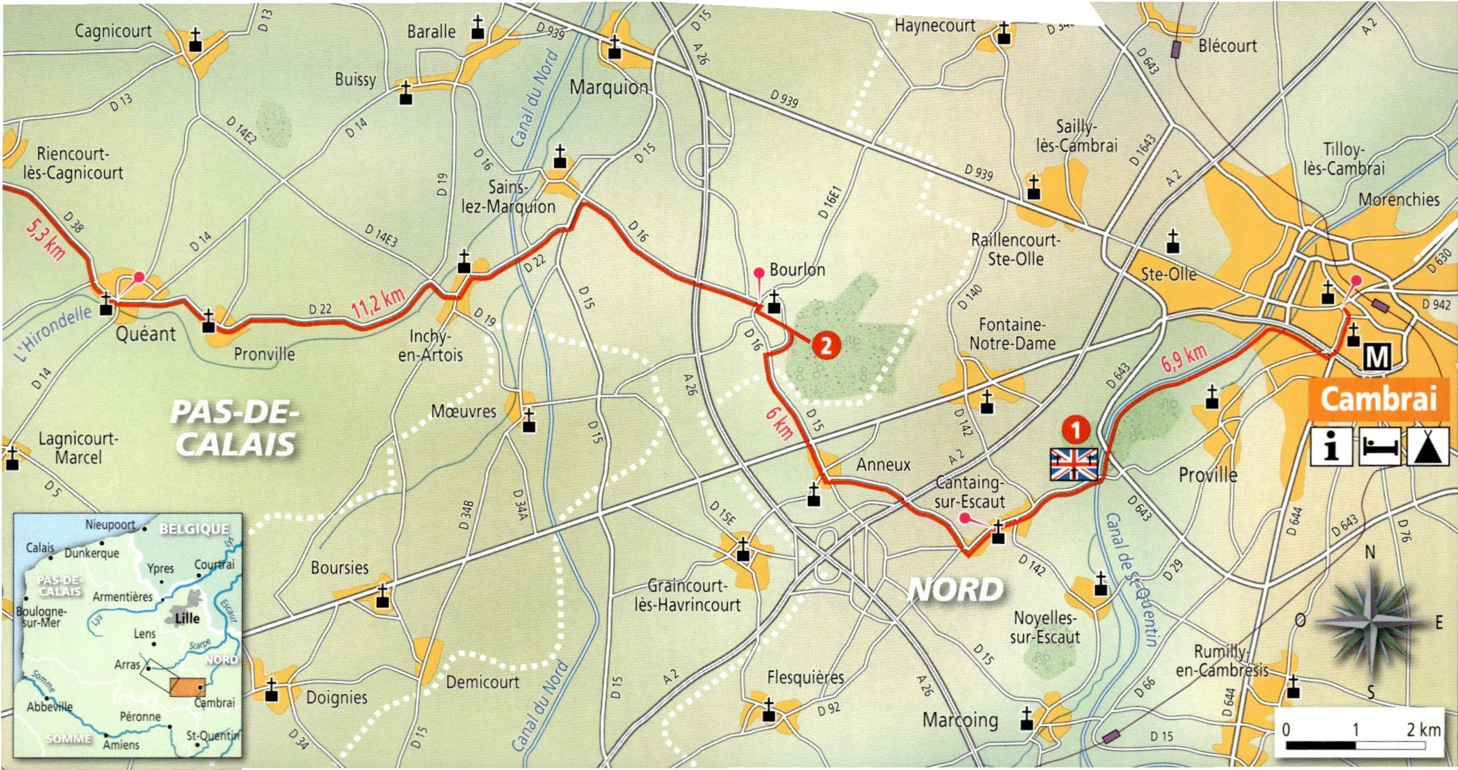
Cambrai
Cagnicourt
Baralle
Haynecourt
Blécourt
Buissy
Marquion
Riencourt-lès-Cagnicourt
Sailly-lès-Cambrai
Tilloy-lès-Cambrai
Morenchies
Sains-lez-Marquion
Raillencourt-Ste-Olle
Ste-Olle
Bourlon
Quéant
Pronville
Inchy-en-Artois
Fontaine-Notre-Dame
PAS-DE-CALAIS
Lagnicourt-Marcel
Mœuvres
Anneux
Cantaing-sur-Escaut
Proville
Boursies
Graincourt-lès-Havrincourt
NORD
Noyelles-sur-Escaut
Rumilly-en-Cambrésis
Doignies
Demicourt
Flesquières
Marcoing
5,3 km
11,2 km
6 km
6,9 km
L'Hirondelle
Canal du Nord
Canal de St-Quentin
D 13
D 14
D 14E2
D 14E3
D 16
D 16E1
D 19
D 22
D 38
D 939
D 15
D 15E
D 140
D 142
D 1643
D 643
D 644
D 942
D 630
D 76
D 29
D 66
D 92
D 34
D 34A
D 34B
D 5
A 2
A 26
N
E
S
O
0
1
2 km
BELGIQUE
Nieupoort
Calais
Dunkerque
Ypres
Courtrai
Armentières
Lille
Boulogne-sur-Mer
Lens
Arras
Abbeville
Péronne
Amiens
St-Quentin
SOMME
Somme
Lys
Escaut
Scarpe

The Second Battle of Cambrai

The 1918 Battle of Cambrai from 8 to 10 October was an element of the large-scale Hundred Days' Offensive. The battle incorporated many of the newer tactics of 1918. The Canadians entered Cambrai on the first day and the capture was achieved significantly sooner than expected.

◆ Since April 1992 a stunning bronze statue, the Bullecourt Digger, has looked out over the old battlefield where in April and May 1917 the Australian Imperial Force lost 10,000 soldiers, killed or wounded. The statue was officially inaugurated on Anzac Day 1993. Commemorations take place here every year on Anzac Day (25 April).

◆ In front of the church there is a memorial to the Australian and British divisions that fought in the battle. Nearby is the Jean and Denise Letaille Museum – Bullecourt 1917
Rue d'Arras, 62128 Bullecourt – Tel.: +33 (0)3 21 55 33 20 – musee-bullecourt1917@orange.fr.

The Australian Memorial Park.

The First Battle of Bullecourt

From 9 April to 16 May 1917, Canadian, British, Newfoundland, New Zealand and Australian troops attacked German defences on a broad front between Vimy (see stage 6) and Bullecourt. With too much undamaged barbed wire, too few armoured tanks to support the Australian infantry and no artillery to hold the enemy down, there were not enough soldiers left to hold the captured section of the Hindenburg Line when the counter-attack came. The 4th Australian Division lost 3,500 men and the British army later used Bullecourt as an example of how a battle should not be undertaken.

N
E
S
O
Fampoux
Athies
Rœux
Pelves
La Scarpe
Boiry-
Notre-dame
Éterpigny
La Sensée
Remy
Haucourt
Vis-
en-Artois
Monchy-
le-Preux
Feuchy
St-Laurent-
Blangy
St-Nicolas
Arras
Tilloy-
lès-Mofflaines
Beaurains
Achicourt
Mercatel
Neuville-
Vitasse
St-Martin-
sur-Cojeul
Hénin-
sur-Cojeul
Heninel
Wancourt
Guémappe
Chérisy
Le Cojeul
Fontaine-
lès-Croisilles
Croisilles
PAS-DE-
CALAIS
Hendecourt-
lès-Cagnicourt
Cagnicourt
Riencourt-
lès-Cagnicourt
Bullecourt
Queant
Noreuil
L'Hirondelle
8,8 km
4 km
6,4 km
5,8 km
5,3 km
5
4
3
A 26
A 1
D 950
D 42E3
D 919
D 42
D 31
D 33E1
D 33
D 34
D 9E4
D 9E6
D 939
D 37
D 37E1
D 260
D 917
D 60
D 265
D 3
D 5
D 9
D 956
D 38
D 13
D 10E
0
1
2 km
Nieupoort
BELGIQUE
Calais
Dunkerque
Ypres
Courtrai
PAS-DE-
CALAIS
Armentières
Boulogne-
sur-Mer
Lille
Lens
Arras
NORD
Scarpe
Escaut
Lys
Somme
Abbeville
Péronne
Cambrai
St-Quentin

The Second Battle of Bullecourt

Preparations were made for a second attack. After intense artillery bombing the village was destroyed but the German resistance was not broken. The charge came on 3 May and the fighting lasted until 17 May. When the Germans withdrew to a new position the British 7th Division held the village and the Australians were in possession of most of the double defence line between Bullecourt and Riencourt. The cost to the 1st, 2nd and 5th Divisions was 7,000 men.

❹ From Bullecourt you ride 12.2km to Monchy on country roads because the D939 does not have a cycle lane and is very busy and unsafe for cyclists.

◆ The Caribou faces towards the objective set for the two Newfoundland battalions, a hill known at the time as Infantry Hill. The attacking units found themselves pinned down by the German counter-attack but the Newfoundlanders pressed on. German counter-attack battalions were swiftly deployed. With only a dozen soldiers, Lieutenant Colonel Forbes-Robertson managed to hold his position for 11 long hours. An artillery barrage was then organised and reinforcements finally arrived to release the pressure and secure this position.

❺ From Monchy it is a gentle 4.2km ride to Fampoux where you join the towpath along the river Scarpe for a flat 8km ride to the town of Arras.

◆ Back in Arras the 720km ride of this section of the Western Front comes to an end.

The "Slouch Hat" Memorial.

The village of Monchy-le-Preux had been taken a few days earlier by the 37th Division and their memorial is a short walk away from the Caribou.

The author's website:

1914-18

www.cyclingthewesternfront.co.uk

Editions OUEST-FRANCE
Lille - Rennes

Editor Hervé Chirault
Editorial coordination Claire Martel
Design Éditions Ouest-France studio
Page layout and photo-engraving Graph&ti, Cesson-Sévigné (35)

ISBN 978-2-7373-6318-4 • Publisher number 7422.01.01.04.14
Legal deposit: April 2014
Printed in Spain
www.editionsouestfrance.fr